THEY ESCAPED FROM HELL

By the same author:

THEY ESCAPED
FROM HELL

by

FRANK JENNINGS

Ex-President National Brotherhood Movement.
Chaplain to the British Circus Ring. Hon. Chaplain to Her Majesty's Forces.

Published by
ARTHUR JAMES
THE DRIFT, EVESHAM, WORCS.

MADE AND PRINTED IN GREAT BRITAIN BY PURNELL AND SONS, LTD.
PAULTON (SOMERSET) AND LONDON

DEDICATION

To all those Christian friends in Australia, New Zealand, India, Japan, America and other far-off countries who freely gave me their love and fellowship. I treasure the privilege of being my Lord's ambassador to people of various races, classes and colours and am supremely happy to record these wonderful miracles of His saving love in human lives.

Contents

STOP PRESS!

O N HIS recent election to become International Leader of the Salvation Army, Commissioner Coutts, who for the past six years has been Chief of the Army in Eastern Australia, was approached for his comments on this book.

He warmly endorsed the retiring General Kitching's Foreword by commending the book to all.

THE SALVATION ARMY
International Headquarters,
London.

October, 1963.

Foreword
by General Wilfred Kitching

I AM sometimes asked by newspaper reporters what I consider to be the most wonderful thing in the world today. Without any hesitation I always reply—the miracle of conversion.

Here in this volume is every evidence, in story form, of the truth that no matter how low a man may sink in sin and despair there is a power greater than these that can lift him up, and when such continue to walk in the path of righteousness that provides conclusive evidence that the omnipotent power of God does restore.

I commend this book with its stories if for no other reason than the confirmation of what I have already said, but it should be a challenge also to all who are interested in the extension of Christ's Kingdom; and there is still need for all of us to remember the constantly repeated phrase of William Booth, "Go for souls and go for the worst." It is by such zeal and faith we best please the Saviour of the World.

WILFRED KITCHING,
General.
International Leader of
The Salvation Army.

London,
  1963.

Introduction

VERY often I am asked by editors of religious newspapers and magazines to permit them to re-use stories and articles in my various books. In the face of such appealing requests one can only grant permission readily and freely.

One such earnest entreaty came by the morning's post. It was from the editor of *The Challenge*, a forthright newsy evangelical weekly published in the city of Auckland, New Zealand. The Editor signed himself "Keith Rimmer", a man I was soon privileged to know very intimately, one whose sterling Christian character and unceasing selfless service was thankfully recognised and honoured throughout the whole Dominion and far beyond. With the letter came an added appeal which warmed my heart.

"Your books meet a great demand over here. Many are won to the Lord through them. Is it possible for you to pay us a visit and conduct a series of meetings some time in the near future?"

Succeeding correspondence led to a committee of Christian friends arranging a series of engagements for me in the larger New Zealand cities, a committee comprising members of most of the churches, as well as those representing the Salvation Army and undenominational missions. The way opened up for me to visit other countries in that far-flung quarter of the globe, invitations to visit India, Ceylon, Aden, Australia, Hong Kong, Hawaii, Japan,

Canada and America, to speak and preach to manifold Christian organisations, to hold devotional retreats and to conduct evangelistic and spiritual healing campaigns. In all, my ministerial tour lasted eight months.

In Christ there is no East or West, no age group, class distinction or colour bar. Wherever there are human beings, there too is to be found redemption, joy and peace through surrender to Him. His eager feet hasten along the dusty streets and highways to meet the essential needs of men. His body was broken in sacrificial love that all people everywhere might be free in the amplitude of that brotherhood which binds them together in the One Father —God. This same Jesus Whose compassionate hands touched life with healing, Whose lips taught men the secret of life and the way to God, was the glad exhilarating theme of my message wherever I went on my daily journeys in those far Eastern countries. Always in my ministry, at home or abroad, I have had as my supreme aim, to strengthen the hands of local ministers, to up-build Christians spiritually and to save souls.

This book deals with people I have met, companioned with and ministered to. As is my usual practice, in the large towns and cities in which I held meetings, I probed their Skid Row areas, that is the squalid, pestilential region where the drunken, poverty-marked human dere-licts eke out a sordid, degrading existence. These pauper-ised, ill-starred down-and-outs, wallowing in their debasing foulness and dirt, are God's children and I wanted to tell them so. So, often when my religious services were over I doffed my ministerial attire, put on some old clothes and went out to talk, eat and sleep with them. I spent many nights in Salvation Army Hostels, Rescue Missions, Harbour Lights, and doss-houses in Melbourne, Sydney, Wellington, Los Angeles, Denver, Chicago and New York, with my sinning, suffering brethren. In the morning, over a simple meal, I quietly told them about my Lord and endeavoured to win them to His love and service. I am happy to say that in some cases I succeeded. These men found new life and happiness in the sheltering arms of God and are now linked up with missions and churches, living upright, godly and sober lives.

The greatest, supremely tragic fact confronting mankind today is the *universality of sin*. It is history's most vicious criminal, the world's biggest and most conscienceless tyrant. It has killed more men than have fallen in all the wars of mankind. It has made smooth the downward path for multitudes, weakened the strong, caused the wise man to be a fool and trampled the fool in his folly. Having made havoc with the lives of millions, its sole purpose is to ruin millions more. Our newspapers are full of such sordid stories.

In establishing daily contact with the flotsam and jetsam of humanity who drift in and out of mission halls, flop-houses and free shelters, I found myself inevitably contending with this stupendous, challenging problem of human sin. Many of those I mated with, deep-down in their hearts, detested their sins and wished to be free of them. But sin is truly, mercilessly powerful. These debased, pitiable people, although often thoroughly ashamed of their varied sins, found themselves unable to be free of them. Weakly they hugged them close until their whole lives were poisoned by them. I came to hate their sins but to love the sinner. Eagerly I told him that I had the positive remedy for his sin, the definite answer to his problem. To him and his evil-tainted kind, to my congregations in churches and halls, my constant word was that the ever-new Christ-centred Gospel which declares the infinite possibilities for the redemption of man is gloriously true, that

Christ Himself, through His dynamic love and mercy, does seek and find the lost, does rescue the perishing and does uplift the fallen. So that when there is a religious recovery there will of course be a moral, mental and physical recovery.

From my case-book of Christian conversions, conversions of individuals whom I met on my Pacific journey, who were co-operative enough to acquaint me with the salient facts of their life history, I have selected a few stories of lives miraculously transformed by the saving power of Jesus Christ. Here is first-hand, not hearsay, evidence of what I know to be true. Drunkards, libertines, thieves, down-and-outs, as reported here, realised the greatest truth in this world. When they were in bondage, helpless, needy, afflicted, Jesus came to their aid. Then they experienced release, peace and victory.

That is the thrilling, romantic story of Christianity. Christianity is Christ, His revealing, working power, grace and love. He has never stopped working miracles. In forty-four years of ministry, in very many countries, I have seen Him take the most unpromising material in sin-stained men and women, and remake them in moral and spiritual beauty, honour and radiance. So much so that old-time companions and associates have been driven to say—"We never saw it in this wise."

When we realise that Christ Jesus is actually with us throughout our days, that the divine promises are strictly true, that none can come to Him in vain; when we accept His loving forgiveness for sin of every kind, then we shall enter into the new, resplendent, victorious life. We shall then begin again, clean and pure and sanctified, endowed with His strength to live a life replete with righteousness, purpose, devotion and service, both to God and man.

I love that well-known hymn—"God holds the key to all unknown and I am glad." My Christian faith holds firmly to the belief that although at times God's ways are mysterious, they are more often than not beautifully transparent with caring love and guidance. I believe that that warming invitation which came to me from Christian friends in the Commonwealth was strongly linked with the guidance of God. He, I am certain, arranged that I should *meet again* on Australian shores, the prisoner I had met in an English jail, the man who was now my fellow labourer in the Lord, who had so much to offer me in his burning zeal for Christian righteousness and service. I record his transforming life story in Chapter One.

On the headstone of a saintly friend of mine, at his express wish, are these ennobling and challenging words: "O let me commend my Saviour to you." In death as in life he desired his Christian witness to continue.

I have written this book to exalt my Lord, to recount my testimony to His emancipating, saving and keeping Power, to recommend Him to others. "Hallelujah, what a Saviour!"

Chapter 1

JESUS SAID: "I AM THE DOOR."

"THANKS for the broadcast, padre! You've lived an intensely full and colourful life, haven't you? Can I ask your interest in a task I've undertaken? I've made myself responsible for getting speakers for the women prisoners in Holloway Jail. Every Thursday evening they have a talk on some subject of topical interest. I would be very grateful if you could spare an evening to speak to them on some of the fascinating people you've ministered to for many years. What you were telling us tonight about gypsies or circus folk would, I'm sure, be just the thing and would be greatly appreciated by them."

In his London Langham Place office, after I had appeared again in the Saturday evening programme, "In Town Tonight," the B.B.C. announcer zealously elicited my support for his ennobling contribution to humanitarian service. Gladly I spoke to the prison women on "My Ladies Of The Circus" and felt afterwards that I had brought a little cheer and inspiration into their drab, sequestered lives.

A few days later I was asked to speak to the male prisoners in Wandsworth Jail on some of my experiences among "gentlemen of the road". To that very attentive audience of nearly a thousand men I expressed the hope at the end of my talk that after their prison release they would cultivate the elevating friendship of One Who ardently desired them to spend their lives in the fruitful service of doing good rather than in wasting them within the dismal confines of a prison cell.

Following the meeting, some of the men, with the permission of the warders, were allowed a brief word with me. One of them gave me a surprise by stating that he had heard me preach in my Essex town, the place of his birth as well, that he had been to the same Sunday school in which I was brought up. Stating his name I recalled his godly parents, his father having been a lay preacher and Sunday school teacher. Shocked by my companion's choice of an evil career and for the sake of his greatly respected family, I readily acquiesced in his appeal for me to see him again. From the prison chaplain I elicited full particulars of his criminal record, one that included theft, forgery and hold-ups.

Wandsworth Jail is a massive, forbidding block of buildings situated in South London. As in most prisons it has strong tiers of cells, one on top of another, connected by an iron staircase. Along a stone corridor at the far end of the second floor I found my man. One other prisoner was with him in the cell. Helpfully he went to bed leaving me to concentrate on his partner whom I had come expressly to see. We shook hands warmly.

"What is your Christian name, my friend?" I asked.

"Call me Jack," he replied. "I wasn't christened that, but it's what all the underworld boys call me. I've got used to it which is just as well. I'm not anxious to throw my real name about."

"Why not?"

"Would you, if you had my rotten past? I bet you wouldn't." He spoke brusquely and arrogantly.

"My friend, I'm glad I haven't your past. I'd call myself a downright fool if I had. The Christian faith helps to keep a man's footsteps on the straight and narrow path, you know. It's got the common-sense brand on it. What's to stop you going in for it?"

"Blimey, you're a real Bible puncher, aren't you? Lose no time in selling your religious wares, I must say."

He made a sneering sound and shook his head negatively. I sat down on the edge of the lower bed and motioned him to sit beside me. Then I fixed his eyes firmly.

"You asked me to come and see you. What for? I've come a good way to honour my word. What do you expect me to talk about? Prison regulations or the supposed toughness of the warders or the political situation?"

"Of course I don't," he replied spiritedly. "But with all respect to you, I don't believe in this religious business. I'm simply not interested in Christianity or the Church. Why—Christianity doesn't fit the facts of truth today. It's full of old myths and fables only suited for the ignorant. People who think for themselves are getting free from those old time-worn religious shackles. Since I've been in 'jug'—prison to you—I've read a good number of free-thinking books by people like Robertson and Spencer and Foote. Why—they easily demolish the case for Christianity. Without it you can go forward to increasing knowledge and progress."

He looked at me with a cold appraising eye, suspicion and enmity oozing from every pore.

"So! You had to come to prison, to kick over the traces of law and right living, in order to learn that Christianity is one big fake, a world fraud that's duped millions of people throughout the centuries! That's it, is it? My friend, forgive me for saying so but you are talking utter balderdash. You're very much out of your depth, you know, and much out of date both with your reading and your thinking. Have you truly given this subject much serious consideration? Frankly, I don't think you have. Seems to me you've been spending your spare time here reading shoddy, ill-digested stuff published by the secularist press. When did you read the New Testament last? When did you seriously study the Bible? Tell me what book you have read on Christian evidence! I strongly doubt whether you have ever read a single book of that kind. You're just repeating foolish jibes against the Christian faith you've heard atheists and rationalists say."

My voice sounded rather loud in that small cell for I spoke with a show of impatience because of the conceited, cocksure attitude of my companion. He stood up and faced me.

"If I was a Christian like you I'd give it up because look at the state of the world today despite the fact that we've had Christianity in the world for two thousand years."

He waved his hands about as if the very thought of the Christian faith was an idle and contemptuous one.

"We've had the proclamation of the message of Christianity in the world for two thousand years," I answered, "but has the world received it and heeded it? Have succeeding generations done so? Have you tried it? We've had cattle in the world for two thousand years yet lots of people are still vegetarians. The present state of the world, its crime, cruelty and injustice, is solely due to the myriad of folk who won't work out the implications and commandments of the Christian faith. Can't you see that?"

He strode about the cell impatiently, then returned to me.

"Garn, it won't work," he said impetuously. "It won't work because there's nothing to it."

"How do you know?" I replied. "Are you an authority on it? Can you honestly put your hand on your heart and say—'I've tried this thing for myself and I firmly declare that it's all eye-wash and bunkum.' Can you?"

He ejaculated fiercely.

"I don't need to try it. I've already told you. It's all me eye and Betty Martin. It's squash and bilge and a lot more. You'll never get modern, intelligent people to accept it."

I got up from the bed, placed my hand on his shoulder and looked him straight in the eyes.

"My friend," I said quietly, "I'm very sorry for you. I'm sorry because you speak like an ignorant man. Do you realize that had you given the Christian faith some real serious thought, had you genuinely studied the life and ministry of Jesus, had you whole-heartedly heeded His personal challenge to you, that in every probability, you wouldn't be here, in this unattractive cell just now wasting precious years of your life. Christianity doesn't send a man to prison. It serves to keep him out of it. It strengthens a man in his weakness and helps him to face and overcome evil. That's plain, proved, every dot-and-comma truth. You give Christianity a fair, thorough-going trial and you'll soon find its beneficial effects on your whole personality."

"Not me," he sneered. "Like most people I can do without it. I can paddle my own canoe."

"Can you—successfully? Does your presence here as a caged-in man prove that? Does it? Let me speak as one who has come here to help you. It definitely appears to me that unless you speedily formulate a new and higher valuation of everyday life, get a clearer conception of your duties and responsibilities as a citizen, you are truly destined to meet a lot more future trouble and to spend many more months in places like this. I feel strongly impelled to talk to you as plainly as this, acquaint you with a few home truths."

He made a snarling noise in exasperation.

"So what?" he exclaimed. "Tell me when you're ready for the collection and I'll take it."

It was abundantly evident that I was wasting my time, being mocked for the pains I had taken in coming to see him. He wasn't big enough in mind and manners to appreciate the purpose of my visit. The sinner was fettered by his repulsive sin.

"I'm going now," I said quietly. "I feel I ought not to leave you without a word of prayer, to ask God to do what I can't. What about it?"

"Please yourself! I'm not stopping you! If you want to pray, go ahead. Only you'll be talking to yourself, mind. It won't affect me. I can see no sense in it."

Regretfully I felt that any prayer of mine might be sneeringly interrupted and ridiculed. I didn't want that to happen. So after a perfunctory handshake, I hurriedly left the prison precincts. The man passed outside the ministry of my care for several years.

Then one day, my eyes fastened on to his name in a newspaper account of a gang raid on a London bank. He was caught with two other thugs. I felt a keen desire to go to his trial at the Old Bailey. Looking at him as he stood in the dock enclosure I was shocked by his changed appearance since last I saw him. He had aged far beyond his years. Conspicuous grooves furrowed his cheeks. Wisps of grey hair straggled untidily over his forehead and ears. His old vigour of smarting sarcasm was now markedly absent. His green-blue eyes had the glint of defeat in them. He looked a time-battered criminal, a scarred physical man, complete with a shrivelled soul.

What a wretched, sorry record the prosecution detailed about him, a horrifying, almost frightening document. From his first crime at the age of sixteen until his last soon after his release from Wandsworth, the tale of fraud, viciousness, and roguery was unfolded, a complete Rake's Progress that revealed a man whose whole being was immersed in all that was dastardly, base, scurvy and vile. If ever an individual played fast and loose with the paramount values which alone keep the world sweet and clean, this reckless prisoner was that person. Seemingly, he respected little and reverenced nothing. He thought he could live successfully on his wits, that his wits were superior to those of the policeman, the magistrate and the judge. In the end, of course, he was utterly and completely trapped in the web of his own spinning. At the end of the prosecution's indictment against him, it was easy to sum up the general opinion of the court that he was "a bad lot".

"Prisoner at the bar," the judge said briefly and sternly. "Your crime list is appalling. Listening to the sad recital of your misdeeds I have been trying to find some evidence of regret coming from you in regard to them, something I could say in your favour. There is none. You have been found guilty of a dastardly crime. If you persist in this evil way of life then you must suffer the consequences. You will go to prison for four years."

The convicted man seemed to shrink and collapse. His face became ashen grey and worked convulsively, revealing his inner turmoil. His lips were parched and his tongue began to curl round them in order to give them moisture. I felt that cold fear was knocking at his heart. He gazed hurriedly round the court, gave me a stare of recognition, turned in company with the two warders on either side of him and disappeared down a back stairway.

More than a year afterwards a letter reached me postmarked "Princetown". I was greatly intrigued concerning the writer and very much surprised and overjoyed when I read the contents of his letter. It was headed Dartmoor, and signed "From a now wiser and repentant prisoner, Jack P., late of Wandsworth."

It began:

> *Nearer, my God, to Thee, nearer to Thee!*
> *E'en though it be a cross that raiseth me.*

There followed words of humble apology for the writer's poor display of rudeness when he met me last in his Wandsworth cell. He assured me that a great change for the good had come over him in the preceding months. He asked me to write to him, and to remember him nightly in my prayers. So began a welcome correspondence with my fellow townsman Jack that brought me heart-enriching delight, a correspondence that eventually was to lead me to meet once again not a despicable, cantankerous convict, but a worthy, buoyant Christian man who, because of his spiritual expression of life and exuberant religious testimony, became a powerful influence for righteousness both inside his prison and outside of it.

Succeeding letters informed me that he had cultivated the companionship of a fellow prisoner who during many years had been in and out of most of the prisons in England. He was a confirmed jail-bird, registering against his name nearly all the heinous crimes a person could possibly commit. It was refreshing to read that during his sojourn in Dartmoor this man had experienced a spiritual cleansing of heart and outlook, had become a stalwart, sunny Christian and was a clean-cut, happy, busy convert, radiating the good cheer of his Master to his prisoner comrades. Among them was my joyous correspondent Jack. He referred to his helpful friend by his nick-name, Dicky the Treadlight.

Challenged by Dicky's complete religious revolution of life, his conduct, speech and outlook, Jack was impelled to give serious thought to his own, to consider what his long list of selfish infamies had brought him. He reviewed the heart poverty and mental misery during the years he had spent in the wilderness of sin, the conspicuous factors that had blinded him to the truth. He boldly confronted himself with the degradation, the disgrace, bitterness and utter hopelessness of his present mode of life. He wrote with shame about his loathsome prison surroundings. They made him detest himself for his asinine weakness of will, his utter inability to go straight when he was free. Many of his fellows-in-crime disgusted him by their cheap arrogance, their plausible boasts that the law would never catch up with them again in their future evil maraudings. In them and their idle words and swaggering attitudes he saw his own past and foolish reflection. He had now much time to think, to survey the years of yesterday. Memory troubled him persistently, keeping alive the constant, anti-social misdeeds he had done and the many people he had so sorely sinned against when he was in the freer and wider world outside his restricting prison ones.

The outstanding, incontestable thing that mightily impressed him was the radical change in Dicky the Treadlight's life. He knew that his greatly esteemed friend had been a hardened criminal, a conscienceless rotter and besotted drunkard. Yet, all at once, he had abandoned these deeply-ingrained vices and become virtuous and law-abiding. In the solitude of his cell, locked in, cramped and lonely, Jack reflected on the miracle of Dicky's conversion. How came it about that a hardened criminal could suddenly undergo a startling life-change, be morally and spiritually illumined?

"For many weeks I have thought about it," he wrote to me in an early letter. "I've been really baffled, quite unable to see any sense in it. I've always regarded most religious people as softies, going in for religion because they were afraid of death and what happened afterwards. But Dicky! He's been a man, a real man, not afraid of anyone or anything. Yet here he is day by day, talking to me and others about Jesus Christ, about prayer, and going straight, cutting out of life swearing and boozing and robbing and a lot more under-the-knuckle things. He talks like some old parson and has me fairly jiggered. But there it is. Facts are facts. Dicky is changed. There's no getting away from it. All the boys here know he's turned religious and most of them respect him for it although they don't jump on his gospel wagon. I'll tell you more in another letter."

He did. Very soon afterwards I received a memorable, gladdening message informing me that he had followed the example of his friend Dicky and turned over his badly-stained life to the Saviour Christ. He put it in these words:

"Dicky has shown me conclusively that if I had any sense of decency at all I should stop hitting others below the belt. You know, robbing and coshing them, sending them to hospital and injuring them. Once I didn't care how much harm I did to others so long as I got my own way. Now I do. I've gone right about face. I've been with Dicky as often as prison regulations have allowed and asked him all sorts of questions about religion. He got me a New Testament, a book I hadn't read since I was a kid. I found it fascinating and it began to get me. I asked Dicky about those verses that spoke to me personally. 'Come unto Me and I will give you rest.' 'As the Father has loved Me so I love you.' 'Go and sin no more.' You know them. Gradually I felt a change inside me. I wanted to be different, turn away from my old life and begin again. God became very real to me. The thought came to me—if God can save Dicky, He can save me. He has now done so. I'd never prayed in my life but the other day I had to. I was desperate. On my knees, in this cell here, I asked God to help me and I handed over my life to Him. Fancy me a Christian! Now I'm trying like Dicky, to bear my Christian witness and am not disappointed with the result."

My friend Jack thereafter became a model prisoner and earned many remission marks. Until his freedom, his letters breathed the warmth of good cheer and the exhilaration that comes from joyous Christian discipleship. After his prison release he told me that many of his jail companions thanked him for his spiritual testimony while others scoffed and said: "When you get outside you'll soon forget that 'Holy Joe' bilge. The cops will nab you on your first job. You'll be back, you'll see."

On the glad afternoon of his jail discharge from Dartmoor I eagerly awaited him at Paddington station and took him to my London home. For several days he was my happy guest. How greatly I esteemed his warming companionship and enriching Christian testimony! Without doubt or scruple he was a man whose heart and life God had manifestly touched. Instinctively I knew that my friend, who had known the harsh tide of battle and defeat, was now more than a conqueror over the majority of the heinous sins that formerly so easily beset him. He commended his Christian faith by his winsome character, giving me and other of my vagrant companions in my care kindly words of counsel and encouragement.

When we were alone in the privacy of my study he poured out his soul to me in positive eagerness and relief.

"You know, padre," he said on one occasion, "the devil is an old sweater. You slave for him as I've done for many years and he repays you badly. Look what he did to me! He encouraged me to fool my brains away and led me into a world of unhappiness, crime and insecurity. He beat me down and gave me an evil-marked face, rotten thoughts and striped clothes. He landed me in prison with no home, no friends, no savings. He gloated when I told him my life was maimed, that he had shackled me with chains of stupid folly. Yet there are some who say there's no devil. Well, he got hold of me all right. I know there's a hell because I've lived in it for years."

Several talks of this fruitful kind we had together. For many hours we discussed the spiritual transaction that had been accomplished in his life. Revealingly, the Master Specialist took charge of him and, as a result, there was no happier mind-and-soul man than my worthy friend Jack.

One never-to-be-forgotten October evening I got him to speak to the members of my week-night service in my then London Stamford Hill Church.

"Jesus Christ has saved me from my sins and from myself," he began. "There was a time in my life when I was plainly a human beast. Nothing was too bad for me to do. For years I carried a razor in my breast pocket always ready for use on the slightest provocation. Also I had a sharp dagger which enabled me to get my way with quite a few of my victims. Now I carry my Bible which, as you know, is sharper than a two-edged sword. I have learned to count more and more on my Saviour, and in consequence, I have now a heart peace in place of my previous restlessness. God Who for years, was just a name to me, is now very close and very real. I am conscious of His love and guidance. I've been degraded and punished for my sins. Why am I now a Christian? What did it? Who did it? Out of my own experience I can tell you that Jesus Christ reached down to hell to save me. He thought me worth saving. He did it. I have told you something of my story because I want others to profit by my very foolish life. He can save you too if only you will fully surrender your lives to Him."

I was glad to have among my church folk a living witness to miraculous conversion. It is wonderful what God can do with a sinful life if the sinner will but give Him the chance.

Jack became a packer in a London book firm. He was busily engaged many week-nights and on Sundays speaking in various churches, halls and clubs, sharing with his audiences his own story of what Christ had done for him. He had several converts and told me that he had never known such happiness.

Nearly two years passed in which God used him mightily in strengthening His kingdom on earth among men. Often we had fellowship together in my own home and in mission campaigns I was engaged in, during which I was glad of his help in speaking and counselling. He developed into a powerful, convincing advocate for his beloved Lord.

One eventful night he burst in upon me, his face suffused by a contagious smile. He wasted no words in a preliminary explanation.

"I'm going to Australia," he said gaily. "I've been reading in *The Christian* and *The Life of Faith* about the need of preachers and evangelists out there and I've been in touch with Australia House and they said I can get an assisted passage if I go and stop for a few years. So I've been praying a lot about it and God has laid it on my heart to go. I can get some ministerial training in one of the Bible schools there and I'm willing to go anywhere. If they'll send me as an evangelist to the people living out in the bush—my, I'll go like a shot."

My friend Jack went to the Commonwealth. Succeeding letters from him told of immense satisfaction derived from theological education in a Bible Institute and of his ministry to a group of bushrangers in the interior.

I have thought much since about my friend, the once evil-living man who eagerly turned his back on the prison shades of Dartmoor and walked towards the light and love of the Cross of Christ, the once wild and reckless individual who was lifted out of the gutter of slime and given a new heart and life by the loving Spirit of Jesus Who transforms all and everything for good. Solely because of his new Master he is now leading others from the darkness of sin to the light of abiding virtue. Because of my friend Jack's miraculous conversion I often read with a new and personal affection the truth-filled promise—"When the enemy shall come in like a flood, the Spirit of the Lord shall lift a standard against him." That's the standard of the Cross, the banner of the Crucified One.

And I was to meet Jack again!

Chapter 2

JESUS SAID: "WHOSOEVER."

WHEN the invitation reached me from Christian friends in New Zealand to visit their vigorous country, my thoughts instantly travelled to Australia where my good friend Jack was labouring hard and successfully among diggers and navvies out in the bush. I longed anxiously to see him, to offer him the hand of support and encouragement in his ministerial labours. In the succeeding weeks, God opened up a way for me not only to visit Australia, but also to spend several uplifting hours in the stimulating company of my old friend who came a long way from his bush station to meet me in the city of Fremantle.

Looking earnestly upon him as he came forward rapidly to meet me, I thought instantly of the Master's exhilarating words, "I have told you these things that my joy might be in you and that your joy might be full." Jack's whole personality was stamped with inner joy. His rugged face was literally shining with infectious gaiety and contentment. There was a rollicking assurance in his firm tread that re-assured and convinced me that he had unquestionably discovered the secret of enriching and satisfying life. Smartly dressed in a grey suit, collar, tie and velour hat, I marked him as one eager for religious adventure, one who revealed a complete devotion to his newly-found Lord. He gripped my hand tightly. The laughter in his heart was reflected in his lustrous eyes.

"The Lord's Name be praised," he said earnestly. "Fancy us meeting out here! Who'd have believed it. What hath God wrought! I'm delighted to see you again, sir."

We had a hurried meal together in a near-by restaurant. There were many questions I wanted to ask him concerning his life in Australia and his ministry in the backwoods.

"Jack," I said eagerly, "time is going to dog our feet much too closely for our satisfaction. Tell me something about your pastoral labours, the people you deal with, the response to your message. Now that you're an oracle of God, a fellow-partner with me in building up His earthly kingdom, how do you find things in your Christian field?"

He sat back and laughed heartily.

"An oracle! I like that. Isn't that something to do with a wise man? Well, I'll say this much. I haven't a big commodity of brains but I'm wise enough to accept and preach what I know to be true. I've served the Prince of the Power of Darkness for far too many years as you well know. He let me down with a big bump. I suffered much at his hands. Now I've got a new boss. I've swung over to the Lordship of Christ, One Who loves me and gave Himself for me. I've committed myself wholly and eternally to Him. I owe the fun, the solid happiness I get out of life to Him and I've pledged myself to be His man until I come to rest at last at His feet. You know my constant testimony? I sing and recite it almost daily.

> *From sinking sands He lifted me,*
> *With tender hands He lifted me,*
> *From shades of night, to plains of light,*
> *Oh, praise His name, He lifted me."*

He paused for a moment, threw his head up and grinned at me happily. Then, in a positive and enthusiastic manner, he went on to tell me about his pastoral labours among his scattered congregation—gangs of navvies, tree-fellers, farmers and isolated communities. In an aged, dilapidated car, he travelled from ranch to village, from hamlet to sheep station, holding services in shacks, halls, farm barns, home kitchens and in the open air. A large thinly-populated territory was his parish. His buoyant faith in God grew greater as his selfless service extended to people of any age, colour and creed. He embraced his adored Lord fervently as he touched the lives of men, women and children he encountered in scattered homesteads in the wide open spaces. What a privilege, he affirmed, was his to preach the salvation glory of Jesus Christ to all who would listen to him.

"You see," he went on, "I know I have the big basic truths of our life and age to declare to my hearers, the truths which will solve all pains and problems, heal the universal wounds, truths which, if accepted, will cause people to grow in the image and likeness of Christ which is their eternal birthright and heritage. I've found the life-changing love of my Saviour shining through the personalities of many of my folk. They're lovable, sincere people offering a love and a faith to others that's a constant challenge to me. Their lives blaze in Christ's service."

He took a dusty Bible from his pocket, turned the pages quickly to St. John's Gospel, chapter one. Firmly he read out, "As many as received him, to them gave he power to become the sons of God, even to them that believe on his name."

"That's it!" he exclaimed. "That's my Christian testimony. Christ is as real to me today as He was when He came to me in prison. I simply could not now live without Him. I feel Him very near to me, having the blessed assurance that His hand is upon me and on all I undertake in His name. I'm a big sinner saved by grace and I know

B

I've been called by my beloved Lord out of blackest darkness into His marvellous light. Oh, how I praise Him? But for Christ where should I be to-day? Still rotting away, morally and spiritually, in the close confines of a prison cell. Just that. I was dead to all things decent. Now I am alive, born into a new world. He has given me something better than money, ease and position. He has given me the privilege of sharing His love with so many. What joy and peace is mine! Padre, my life is staked on the greatest truth in the world. I've got my hands on reality. I'm always making mistakes but they're not as before my conversion, from evil intent. Oh no! I sometimes put a foot wrong but so long as I tell others about my Lord, able to give them a moral and spiritual rebirth, I can never put a soul wrong. The road to abiding happiness, universal brotherhood and service is not by politics, economics and philosophy, but by the utter giving of ourselves to the will of God through faith and love in Jesus Christ. That's eternal, effective truth and I'm going on to preach it until my dying day. My times, my life are in His hands."

He stopped speaking, smiled at me, then closed his eyes for a brief moment as if saying within himself—"God bless that testimony!"

I looked into his bronzed and weather-beaten face. It was jovial with wholesome friendliness and Christian certainty. I knew that his life was hid with Christ in God. Marking his spiritual growth, his enthusiastic Christian witness, I found it difficult to remember that *this* was the man who but a few years before had insolently snarled at me from the dismal precincts of an English jail and complacently wore the repellent garb of a prison convict. When all seemed lost, when he seemed doomed to spend all his days as a wretched felon, he called on God to free him from the stranglehold of sin and degradation.

With what result? God reached down to him, snapped his hellish fetters and led him into a new universe of reality and love. Here was a radiant, Christ-filled man who was appealingly and strongly indifferent to home comfort, wealth, power or fame, to whom now, the world spread its allurements in vain. I know he was a dweller on God's mountain-tops, where the view is clear and beautiful.

Leaving him to hold a brief fellowship with other Christians in the city I thought much of the supreme miracle of Christian conversion. What is it? It's a Christ-power that changes a man's life from misery to joy, from filthiness to cleanliness, from darkness to light, from death to life. My friend Jack had found the life pearl of great price. With spiritual faith, courage and gaiety, he stepped out to adorn human existence with a solid captivating Christ-filled service which he shared with others.

Some days later I paced up and down the deck of the P. & O. liner *Himalaya* as she narrowed the strip of water that separated us from the harbour of Melbourne. Impressive white-foamed ocean rollers flooded all around us from the mighty Pacific. Winding in and out of long streets of the city I could see inviting inland bays, magnificent surf beaches and golden sands. My eyes focused too on many fine public buildings and large business stores.

What awaited me in this capital city of Victoria? Its main thoroughfares thronged with people who, on business or pleasure bent, elbowed and jostled each other with careless indifference. Were they interested in the Christian message? Would they listen to a preacher from England? Among them, I was certain, were many who, at one time, walked with Jesus, but now to their own hurt, had wandered away into the far country and denied themselves His stimulating companionship. Could I possibly get hold of some of them, tell them what my Lord commissioned me to say to them, that to all returning prodigals, He gives the best robe and a ring and all the privileges of sonship, as though they had never left Him!

And to the human derelicts, that large army of destitute and homeless men, meandering to and fro along streets and alleys in search of food, shelter, friendship and security. Had I not a personal, sympathetic word for them? Could I not tell them that I had lived their life for weeks and months at a time in order to try to understand the dire hardship of their poor lot, that all over the world I had companioned with their heavy-hearted, desolate-minded brothers, tramped as a tramp along the dusty highways of England and other European countries, worked my passage across many States of America, sampled the majority of the Poor-Law institutions and their associate shelters for the needy—Rowton Houses, Salvation Army Hostels, Church Army Homes, lodging-houses and free night shelters! Yes, I felt that having "sat where they sat", my sharing message to them would be all the more freighted with concern and compassion. I would tell them of my London Thames Embankment ministry, of how most Sunday nights for four years during my Old Kent Road ministry, at the close of my evening service, I went along to the grim dormitory of the poverty-stricken on the Embankment in search of the unwanted, there feeding the hungry, offering them an encouraging word and taking some of them back with me to my Camberwell home which, during those God-given years, became a temporary refuge for the penniless and homeless.

What should I say to the Christian friends awaiting me on the quayside? I would tell them that we were not isolated members of a struggling community, but part of the great family of God. We were just one facet of the Church Universal, honoured members of a mighty community gathered up in the universal Fatherhood of God, that His loved Name was Immanuel, God with us, and that, in and through His love and purpose, all barriers of race and nationality and colour were swept away and all distinctions within His vast family made utterly meaningless. All one in Christ Jesus for He is the true and transforming Light of the World. That would be my glad theme to my fellow-Christians patiently waiting to welcome me as their ministerial ambassador from England. It is frequently hard to work for God and not sometimes lose heart, I would tell them. But I would add—"Let us get back to the main issues of our Christian Faith, back to Christ, back to the Life of God which is synonymous with the Love of God. Then things will happen and we shall be revitalised by fresh and continuous contact with Him. Our civilisation needs the practical application of the teaching of Christ as never before. That civilisation will crash unless it tries Christianity before it is too late."

Such were my thoughts as I eagerly waited for the *Himalaya* to dock. When it did so I was soon warmly welcomed by Salvation Army officers, mission workers and devoted Christians from different churches. These dedicated folk were buoyant and gladsome in their religious experience, radiating the spirit of Christian love and cheer that made their lives the most fragrant in the world. It was exhilarating to be in their company, to be sustained by their faith, their courage, their rich and varied experiences of God's grace. After tea I went along to the Salvation Army Citadel and united with friends in singing:

> *What matters where on earth we dwell?*
> *On mountain top or in the dell?*
> *In cottage small or mansion fair,*
> *Where Jesus is, 'tis heaven there.*

Less than a week afterwards I spent the night in the main Salvation Army Hostel for homeless men in the city, the Gill Memorial Home, superintended by a valiant disciple of His adored Master, Brigadier Don Downes.

Chapter 3

My near companion's bed was about two yards from mine. When he turned my way his foul breath penetrated my nostrils and caused me to twist over hurriedly lest I should retch. Constantly his troubled dreams caused him to groan, whimper and shout. On occasions he jerked himself violently to a sitting position, looked round blankly, swore savagely and then threw himself back again into a recumbent position. I thought of the superb rescue and redemptive work the Salvation Army was doing, of how daily, unfailingly, they were reaching out to men such as those who companioned with me in that dormitory. Some of them idly complained and criticised the Army work, yet without any question they found a night's shelter and food for a small sum of money that even the most pauperised among them could easily raise. Only for extreme drunkenness was anyone turned away.

I tried hard to sleep but found it impossible. A strange bed, the close proximity of other sleepers, the impure air in the room, largely accounted for my discomfort.

In the early hours of the morning my bed neighbour struck a match and lit a stub of cigarette. It glowed in the darkness like a small torch. By its reflecting light he saw me watching him. Eagerly he turned with a nod of greeting.

"Not much of a shelter for wayfaring men," he said

39

complainingly in a low voice. His words were well rounded and he spoke in a cultured tone. What was a man of education doing in that crowded hostel for homeless and destitute men?

I determined to further his acquaintance. From the pocket of my coat, which like my waistcoat and trousers was under my pillow out of the way of marauding hands and in the place of a missing bolster, I extracted a cigarette and handed it to him.

"Thank you, my friend," he said. "This is a godsend after picking up fag butts in the gutter. Very kind of you." He lit it from the tiny stub he held between his fingers then lay back and watched the spiral smoke as it left his mouth.

My own reason for being in that Salvation Army night shelter in the Australian city of Melbourne was two-fold. I wanted first-hand evidence of how the Australian derelict lived, his outlook on life, sleeping dens and occasional jobs. Secondly, I had heard that in that particular well-patronised abode there were men whose names and qualifications were well-known, who had come from families of good influence and established position. I was impelled to find out the real reason why they were there. Also, was I not a Christian minister and for many years had lived, tramped, and worked with social outcasts of this kind, established hostels in order to help them in their physical and spiritual needs. Someone had to reveal care and compassion for them, tell them about a much better way of life and of the transforming, saving power of Jesus Christ.

In the early hours of dawn I left my strange bed and wandered round the gloomy encircling streets. Soon after seven o'clock I returned to the hostel for a breakfast snack. By that time the many dormitories had emitted a stream of oddly-dressed, unwashed, battered and broken men.

How like others of their kind I had met in various city
shelters for the poor! Jostling me closely were town and
city offscourings mingling with men of gentle habits, hardened rogues with diffident Ishmaelites. Many of them
were diseased in body. Most of them had faces that registered pathetic defeat and despair. Life seemed to hold
nothing more for them. Sitting at greasy tables or standing
in isolated corners they ravenously wolfed eatables of any
kind. Sundry items of fish, meat or fruit were extracted
from newspaper parcels. Cups of tea and slices of bread
and margarine were bought from the hostel canteen.

I spied my night companion leaning against the grimy
door. His appearance was deplorable. The clothes he wore
would have disgraced a scarecrow. They were a jumble
of greasy, torn rags of many faded colours. He looked
an old, weary, haggard man. I watched with sick fascina-
tion the incessant jerking of his mouth and jaw muscles.
Out of half-lidded eyes he gazed vacantly downwards, as
if staring at his thoughts. He was a spectre of bitter
remorse and tragedy. I elbowed my way to him.

"Good morning," I said with a nod of recognition. "We
had a word together last night while lying in bed. You
remember! How about a cup of tea?"

His mouth stopped its twitching. His listless eyes were
raised to me and opened wide with new life. A thin nervous
hand gently touched my sleeve.

"Ah yes, my friend," he rejoined quietly. "Let me thank
you again. I don't think I want any tea. I have a little
money left you know. But—I'm afraid."

I looked at his shrunken cheeks. They were the colour
of parchment grey, dulled in blood and exhaustion. A
striking picture of maimed, jaded vagabondage. Every line
of his furrowed face advertised hunger of more than one
kind.

"Afraid?" I replied feelingly. "Of what? Any way I can help you?"

With a sharp intake of breath he made a troubled sound. It was a moan of inner pain that featured his whole personality.

"Afraid, my friend," he said after some moments of distressing silence, "afraid of myself. Afraid that very soon after I leave this tawdry hole I shall spend whatever money I have. There are quite a number of low dives near here and they open early, too early for me." His voice quivered with feeling as he spoke.

His candid, pathetic remark opened a window into his entire personality, explained the reason of his depraved, drunken condition and why he was in that hostel for down-and-outs. As I watched him, his face puckered as though near to tears, his lips trembled. I took his arm.

"Come on," I said sympathetically, glad to escape the hot smell of exhaustion and decay, "you're coming with me. I think we can beat the pubs between us."

We had a simple meal in a small café. The warming food, the companionship of someone whom he said, without then knowing my identity, was "a little bit different to the others," caused him to shed his diffidence, to loosen his tongue in eager comradeship. From that hour a friendship was forged between us, a friendship that saw us together day by day in Melbourne, a friendship that fluctuated in hope and despair, that culminated in the joy of immense pride and thankfulness.

Clifford's father was an Anglican clergyman who for many years worked in a slum parish in London. He had a public school education, and afterwards was articled to a city solicitor. Developing a love for acting, he joined a local dramatic society and then a Midland repertory company. From small parts he progressed until he became a leading man. His fame grew as an actor, and an invitation to join a well-known London theatrical company was accepted with enthusiasm. For a time all went well. Success, in the form of notoriety and an ample wage packet, was in his keeping. He gloried in the spot-light of renown. Then, a streak of folly and ill-discipline revealed itself in his mental make-up. He became easy-going, increased his consumption of alcoholic liquor, married badly and got into heavy debt with money-lenders. These crippling evils soon affected him. His health suffered, his temper became increasingly frayed, he separated from his wife and finally was sacked by the theatrical company after more than once having muffed his lines.

Worse was to follow. As his drinking habits continued so life became an intermittent orgy. Trouble pressed on the heels of trouble. Licentiousness followed drunkenness. He passed from fair lodgings to bad ones. Requests for small parts in numerous theatrical plays met with a curt and often brutal refusal. He degenerated into a drink-sodden, repulsive profligate. It could not be hidden. His efficient sinning habits plainly registered their mastery over him in his bloated, hang-dog face and his ragged clothes.

The day came when he reluctantly heeded the advice of one of his few remaining friends who loaned him money enough to pay for his assisted passage to Australia. In that great and attractive country he found some odd jobs with a goodly wage packet to go with them. He also found that there were plenty of saloon bars in Australia, many inducements for gambling and immorality. He soon became a weak, abject disciple to these and other vices. So once more, like the Prodigal Son, he spent all the money he could get hold of in the "far country". Hopelessness of mind and soul again engulfed him. Melancholy fashioned for him a hideous cage and grim despair became his dread gaoler. To his bitter cost he discovered that the wages of sin are moral, social, physical and spiritual death, that the way of transgressors is hard.

These sombre facts regarding his tragic, chequered life he gradually and painfully shared with me during our successive meetings. His conversation with me was always tinged with acid bitterness. He saw himself as he truly was. He also looked at the man he might have been, honoured, loved, successful. He was truly conscious of fine powers wasted, of golden opportunities destroyed. He had recklessly chased the bubble mistakenly called pleasure, and all through the years had gained nothing but torture and misery.

One day, walking together through a park, clad as usual in tattered threadbare clothes that made him shiver in the biting wind, he suddenly turned and faced me.

"Do you remember," he said sharply, his face a study in agonising remorse, "what the Florentines said about Dante the author of *The Inferno*? 'Ah yes,' they said, 'he's the man who knows what he's talking about. He's been himself in Hell.'"

For some moments the silence between us was heavy. I sensed that a hard, agonising battle was waging within his mind. Then, his face contorted with pain, he halted his step, glared at me and in a grievous, self-pitying voice said sharply: "So have I!"

Another day, in the Salvation Army hostel, he drew from his torn pocket a printed slip of paper. He said he had extracted it from a story in a weekly magazine. With interest I read it.

"There you are, alone! Adrift! No moorings! No sails to turn the wind to your own purpose! No motive power! You're licked!"

I quickly made my comment.

"You're licked—unless . . ."

"How do you mean, unless?" he asked.

"Unless! Hold tightly to that little word, Clifford. That's your word of hope. Unless someone, somewhere, will lend a hand. Unless someone will point the way out of hell. Unless someone will say, 'God loves you, my friend. God has an investment in you.' I know that Someone. You, too, ought to know Him. You have intelligence, brain enough to know that you're sinning against your true self, your best Friend. Clifford, listen to me. I speak for your own good. You will *never* know peace, love and happiness until you come to know Jesus Christ as your personal Lord and Saviour. That's not pious bleating. That's sound common sense. I'm no fool because I talk to you like this. I know what I'm talking about. I've seen very many chaps just like you, all over the world, possessed by numerous hideous demons, living in a literal hell of their own choice. I've seen them rescued, transformed, re-made into respectable, worthy, God-honoured citizens. You too, if you will say the word and make the effort, can join their number. You do know that, I'm sure."

Sometimes, when I talked to him about the Christian faith and asked him to consider the claims of Jesus on his erring life, he showed impatience and sought to change the subject. This time he didn't. He was very quiet. The lines around his mouth were drawn tightly and I felt that his eyes were near to tears. I was impelled to say more.

"My friend," I went on, speaking as quietly and earnestly as I could, "you referred to Dante just now. I'm sure you know something about Augustine, both an outstanding sinner and saint, how evil he was before his conversion. In his *Confessions* he writes something like this. I quote from memory. 'I turned from Thee, O my God. I lost myself among a multiplicity of bad things. I wandered into fruitless acres of sorrow with a restless weariness. I carried about me a shattered and bleeding soul, heavy to be borne, yet where to repose it I found not. Not until I rested in Thee.'

"You know, Clifford," I continued, "that frank, unadorned avowal of a man's tragic, sinful folly could have been written by you—that is, excepting the last sentence. Couldn't it? It suits your life and condition perfectly. This well-known man made a horrible mess of his life. So have you. He was wise enough to stop the rot by owning a new Master. You can do that. With Christ as his Teacher and Friend, Augustine's past sins were wiped out. Jesus gave him a new heart and a new start. That can happen wholly, absolutely to you. So what about it?"

His face bore a look of outrage. Then the irritation drained itself away. He nodded his head in bewilderment.

"A few weeks ago, when I first met you, I would have said 'piffle' had you spoken to me like that. Today, because of our many talks together and because I realise I'm the devil's own mug, I admit you've got something. But it's all right for you. You're not a weak-willed slave as I am. You don't know John Barleycorn as I do. I've fought and struggled with him day and night. But he's a nifty, shifty one to hit. He gets under your belt, tries all the tricks available to put you flat out. Yes, I know what you're going to say. 'Why let him?' Well, I can't help it. He's got me in his power. I want to beat him. God knows I do. But somehow I don't seem able to. He's got me pulverised. Sometimes I get so sick of myself, of my low manner of life, that I wonder if I can produce enough courage to jump in the river and end it all. Once, I went down to the harbour here and looked for some time at the calm water. I thought I heard a voice in it saying—'Come on, you fool of a man. There's peace here. Jump right in.' Then I knew that was the devil in me laughing at my rotten plight. I tell you, I ran from that cursed spot as fast as my weak old legs would carry me. That experience really frightened me. But what can I do? How can I beat this pitiless fiend who's got me in his clutches? Tell me that!"

As I gazed into his dirty, unshaven face with its hollow cheeks and heavy-lidded eyes, I felt a glowing pang of compassion for him. He looked so forlorn and desperate, so ill and unhappy. It was easy to see he was mortally sick. Utterly and mentally he was under the dominance of drink.

I thought it wise to get him into the fresh air, to spend a little more time with him. He seemed anxious to talk to me and more amenable to listen to what I had to say than on some previous occasions. Also I felt that there was a stirring desire within him for a change of life, some sign of penitence for wasted years. In a nearby park we sat closely together on a seat. Taking from my pocket a Bible which I always carry with me, I turned to John's Gospel and, without a further word to my watching companion, began to read the third chapter, pausing deliberately at apt and significant texts.

"And he came to Jesus. And Jesus said, 'Ye must be born again.'" "We speak that we do know and testify that we have seen." "For God sent not His son into the world to condemn the world but that the world through Him might be saved." "Men love darkness rather than light because their deeds are evil." "He that doeth truth cometh to the light." "He that believeth on the Son hath everlasting life."

He met my kindly look with a sheepish grin.

"What's that in aid of?" he asked softly.

"In aid of someone I'm very much concerned about, someone who admits he's just a silly mug, who's insulting his God-given intelligence living this horrible, sewer-grovelling life. In aid of you."

He stroked his chin thoughtfully. Then he squinted his eyes and swallowed hard.

"You're right, you know," he said with conviction. "Honestly, when I think of what I used to be like before this booze slavery got me. When I look at my present condition, at these awful doss-house clothes, at the people I have to hobnob with in order to get a lousy bed and some cheap food. Well, I have to tell you, I ought to tell you, I'm thoroughly ashamed that I've allowed myself to come to this. God, what a life!"

For a further hour we talked together about his spiritual and physical condition. He listened earnestly to what I had to say. I felt that he was sincere when he said he wanted to be and do something different. He kept on referring to his past life, saying that it smelt as foul as his frowsy clothes. Before leaving he promised me that he would make a big effort to keep out of saloons, that any money he earned doing odd jobs after paying for bed and food he would hand over to me to save. Finally he said he would think very seriously over the Christian message and asked me to get him some Christian books. That night, in the Army hostel in Becket Street, Melbourne, I gave him a Bible, a book by an old friend of mine, the late Dr. Sangster, *The Secret of Radiant Life*, and another I had in my case, *The Devil's Playground*, one of my own books dealing with down-and-outs I had met in America, men who had been cleansed from the guilt and stain of their past sins and had received power to live as children of God.

For several weeks after that I saw him almost daily. At various meetings and services I held in neighbouring churches and mission halls in the city he was in my congregation. I managed to get him some decent clothes and with a collar and tie to match, combed hair and shaven face, he looked very smart and attractive. The old languid, hang-dog scowl gradually disappeared. A hovering brightness filled his eyes. I sensed that the ministry of Christian grace was working firmly within his soul. From time to time he handed me money to keep for him. He was holding closely to a dock-labouring job and spending his evenings either reading or in religious meetings rather than in saloon bars. I waited hopefully and expectantly to hear good news about his Christian conversion.

One memorable evening I conducted a service in an undenominational mission in Abbotsford Road. The hall was full of the human dregs of the street, visitors and Christian workers. In a back seat I spied my friend Clifford. The service was intensely stirring and joyful. I finished my address by appealing to everyone present to surrender their lives fully to Jesus Christ, to know the joy of sins forgiven and a future radiant with high purpose and happy service. I announced the closing hymn, "Tell Me the Old, Old Story", and asked again that as we sang it friends would leave their seats and come and kneel at the form provided, in token that they wished to accept Christ as their Lord and Saviour. As we sang the third verse—

> *Remember, I'm the sinner*
> *Whom Jesus came to save,*

Clifford left his seat and walked boldly to the penitent form and there knelt down. Other converts knelt with him. In order to have a long chat with Clifford I decided to stay the night at the mission and was offered a cubicle bed which I gladly accepted. When my friend stepped into my humble bedroom his face just glowed with a new-found radiance. Something evil and tyrannical had left him. Something strong and satisfying had taken charge of him. It was plainly evident that a new happiness possessed him.

"It had to happen," he said with a winning smile. "I've been coming to it for some time. My reading of the New Testament and those books you gave me gradually cleared my head and my eyes. I began to see things in general as well as myself in a proper light. I came to be ashamed of my condition, my boozing habits, the stinking places where I slept, the grovelling moochers I mixed with. Man, how could I sink so low! I came to hate my sins and wanted to be free of them. Then I knew I wanted Christ. Just like that. I knew He was the Key to all my problems and the sooner I accepted Him as my Saviour the better for me and everybody else. So there it is. I've done it."

We talked and prayed together until a very late hour. That small bedroom of mine became literally an annexe of heaven. As he left me I looked into his shining eyes and Christ-suffused face and thanked my God for a regenerating Christian faith that could so radically change a life like his from foulness to purity, from beastliness to blessing.

The letter eventually caught me up some seven months later when I was missioning in America.

"Dear Padre,

Look to your laurels for I too am now a preacher. The Christian friends here have been using me a good deal in their churches and halls since you left. Sunday by Sunday I go round saying a little word for my Lord Who has called me out of horrible darkness into His most marvellous light. I'm thinking of offering myself entirely for the Lord's work. Perhaps the City Mission or the Open Air Mission will take me. I'm ready if and when He wants me. My solemn pledge is this, I will serve Him until my dying day. I owe you very much for your sympathetic help and companionship. I hold you lovingly in my heart and pray nightly that you may be spared to continue your work among 'the submerged tenth.' I love to sing— 'My chains fell off, my heart was free, I rose, went forth and followed Thee.'

God bless. Ever in His joyful service,

Your thankful friend,
Clifford."

Chapter 4

JESUS SAID: "I WILL."

Nოt long after arriving in the Australian city of
Sydney I heard about a popular open-air forum, a
speaker's corner, which was held every Sunday
morning just off one of the main streets. Among other
speakers, I was informed, was a swaggering, political extremist who viciously attacked any Christian advocate who
came to the site to speak, and on more than one occasion
had been summoned for trying to break up religious
gatherings. In past years I have had a close relationship
with many of his kind, on more than one occasion having
debated with them in public. I thought it good for my
education to seek an opportunity to hear this ill-famed
individual, believing that first-hand evidence is better than
second-hand hearsay.

Preaching one Sunday at Earlwood Baptist Church I
was glad of the afternoon break to go along to the open-
air parliament, hoping that this quarrelsome antagonist of
the Christian faith might be on view. I was soon caught
up with a big crowd which idled aimlessly from speaker
to speaker. Listening carefully to many -isms propounded
by various speakers I was often amazed that men could
use a public platform to voice what most intelligent people
would regard as plain, arrant nonsense. Eventually I found
myself among a number of people heckling a political
speaker. This man made a poor show at answering many

questions put to him and gave way to another, who, according to the noisy remarks of my near companions, was the leader of the political team, the man I had come specially to hear.

"It's old Jim himself." "Now we'll get some fireworks." "Hullo, Jim, just come from the Mothers' Meeting? Are you in the choir yet?" These and other less kindly comments were made by those who elbowed me closely. I was soon left in no doubt that the new speaker was in truth, the extremist champion, the arrogant, bitter opponent of all that Christianity and the Church stood for. He was a thick-set, beetle-browed, middle-aged man, dressed in poor clothes that ill-fitted his portly physical frame. He had a stentorian bull voice that could be heard well beyond the extreme confines of the crowd. His whole appearance suggested vigour of mind and resolution of will, the kind of person who was destined to figure prominently in any organisation he joined. He raved rather than spoke. Every sentence very nearly approached a scream. His face became purple and small, blue veins stood out from his forehead and showed on his nostrils. He looked at times demoniacal, his hands waving about in a wild, undisciplined manner, his hair dishevelled with violent movement. He ducked, swayed, cringed, leaned back in a startled manner as if he had seen a ghost or something as terrifying. Then he hurled himself forward, gazed menacingly before him, adopted a pugilistic stance as if determined to show his adversary that he wasn't after all one bit afraid. I watched him earnestly, fascinated by his verbal and physical display. The provocative thought came to my mind that if we preachers revealed a little more earnestness and passion in our sermons and addresses to the people we speak to, maybe they would be more persuaded of our complete sincerity and devotion to the wondrous, transforming power of the Christian message. My atheistic friend had a frail, cheerless brief. We have a virile, enheartening one.

What he actually said was stale, kindergarten stuff. He didn't believe in God. Why should he? When the Almighty presented Himself to him in person, he might change his opinion. To date he had no reason to do so. Belief in God was a fairy tale. He scoffed at the Bible and its teaching. Kid's yarns from an ancient book, he averred. The churches were dry-as-dust conventicles of capitalists. If they were all pulled down, nobody would be any worse. On the vacant sites could be built more schools of learning and entertainment. The country needed more people with brains, not pious goody-goodies. As he raved on he became impertinently blasphemous about Jesus, His life and teaching. He said he was sure that Marx and Lenin were right in their social and political theories, that the Soviet order of society was the best one. The Christian religion, he fulminated, is completely irrelevant. Only the capitalist dust in the eyes of the working classes prevented the workers in the western countries from seeing all this.

How often have I listened to similar insipid, impoverishing rigmarole from materialistic speakers in many open spaces at home and abroad! Just a cold, soulless repetition of atheistic propaganda that exuded from the mouths of many Russians I argued with in Moscow and Leningrad. I heard nothing valuable, liberating, constructive from this very voluble rationalistic advocate and prepared to move away. He must have seen my clerical collar for his uplifted hand pointed in my direction.

"Ha, ha," he shouted, in a full-throated, waspish voice that compelled the attention of all who faced him, "I see a welcome stranger in the camp. Blow me if it isn't a messenger of the Lord. I must seek his company and gain enlightenment concerning the way from earth to heaven."

Hastily he made room for one of his companions and walked round the back of the crowd to meet me as, with some difficulty, I freed myself from the pressing throng. He smiled cynically when we met and without hesitation held out his hand for me to shake.

"I don't suppose you agreed with a lot I had to say but it's good of you to come, mate," he said, his whole bearing suggesting cocksureness. "Glad to talk to you any time, you know."

"My friend," I replied quietly, "don't call me mate. I prefer the term 'padre'. Also may I tell you kindly that in my opinion, you talked a lot of foolish nonsense. I think you ought to read and consider more than you evidently do. I've heard your sort of stuff from every idealogical extremist I've met. There's nothing original or worthy about it."

His face assumed a ferocious expression. He became a picture of devilish rage. There was something very much of the devil in the glare from his eyes.

"I like that," he said with rising anger. "You've got a cheek, you have. Not afraid to speak up, are you? Let me tell you that you're a blind leader of the blind. I'm prepared to debate my opinions against yours any time. There you are, there's the challenge. What about it?"

Feeling persuaded that in some quiet spot I might be able to convince him of the overwhelming truth of the Christian Gospel, of the richer, satisfying fellowship he could have with Christ, in preference to Karl Marx, I told him that I had to return for the evening service at Earlwood but that one evening, convenient to us both, I would be glad to see him in my bed-sitting room at the Sydney Rescue Mission where I was a temporary but happy guest.

On the evening appointed he greeted me affably, seated himself comfortably in the well-worn armchair I had managed to secure for him and proceeded to light a cigarette from a packet he extracted from his pocket. I noticed then his badly-stained nicotined fingers, his pimpled, blood-red face and coarse, sagging cheeks. He waited for me to open the conversation regarding the purpose of our meeting, so after a few explanations about my work in Australia and in that particular mission, I gave him an opening by asking him why he held the views he did. Impetuously he stubbed out his cigarette, leaned forward intently, fixed me with his staring eyes and for a full fifteen minutes, ranted on sundry dogmas of his political creed.

His was a sharing fellowship. It strove for a class-less society. Every individual should live, work and serve for the good of the whole community. All ought to enjoy the same opportunities for education and progress. Wealth should not only be owned collectively but used in common. Under his political system there was no room for pride and power and unfair treatment of the unprivileged nor the exploitation of the many by the few. It denied the necessity of any religion in a modern world. It believed in universal brotherhood. It stressed its overall conviction —each for all and all for each. If the workers of the whole world would only unite, very soon peace, plenty and progress could come among us and every citizen would enter a heaven upon earth.

So he raved on. To listen to him became wearisome. His language increased in wild, reckless statements; his voice boomed more noisy and raucous. His arms were constantly upflung. He looked wildly pugnacious and frequently stabbed a menacing finger at me. His trouble was that he had lost the art of speaking conversationally. I was an audience and once again, he was on his soap box. I waved to him to stop. He nodded viciously then said something that caused me to raise my eyebrows considerably.

"You see," he fulminated, "what it all boils down to is this, we are workers who are out to build a better world."

He stopped speaking, gazed at me in smug satisfaction, seemingly gratified that he had put up an unanswerable case, that his was the only reasonable and conclusive word.

I closed my eyes and rutted my brows so that the significance of his last remark should sink deeply into my mind.

"A better world!" I found myself repeating. "Why, that's the Christian gospel. This better world challenge was the dominant note in the life and teaching of Jesus. That's why He came, why He called His disciples to help Him in His universal task. 'Thy Kingdom come, on earth as it is in heaven.'"

I opened my eyes and smiled at my companion.

"You know," I said softly, "you are trying to steal the Christian theme, but in doing so you are leaving out Jesus. 'The better world' proclamation and ideal, that was the message of the angels to the shepherds telling them why a little baby was coming to be the world's Saviour. 'Good tidings of great joy to all people.' A better world for everybody. Listen to this!

The Spirit of the Lord is upon me,
Because He hath anointed me to preach good tidings to
*   the poor.*
He hath sent me to proclaim release to the captives,
And recovery of sight to the blind,
To set at liberty them that are bruised.

My listening friend butted in with a defensive word.

"No, no, that's Bible stuff. We don't accept the Bible. It's full of old wives' tales and bears no relationship to our age. Religion has no reality for us and we say that any good in it is supplied by the humanist state."

"But Christianity is bigger, more valuable regarding the social, moral and spiritual things of life than the state. Your particular brand of humanism places all its emphasis on material well-being. It is as you admit, frankly materialistic and atheistic. Is there nothing more in life than mere materialism? We are just human, soulless animals grovelling about the earth for a few years and then—'dust to dust, earth to earth' and that's the final end! Just that? You will have great difficulty in convincing intelligent people that we are nothing more than physical clods, that the be-all and end-all of life is the state, and that man is only a means to that end. The big trouble with you and your kind is that you persist in leaving out God. You deny that men need Jesus as the Saviour of the world. Isn't that right, friend?"

He flew into a temper and eyed me scornfully.

"I've already told you what I think about religion," he answered. "It's all eye-wash, all right for hysterical women and feeble-minded men. I don't need it nor do others who use their brains. You speak about God. There isn't a God. He's as dead as mutton."

"Come, come, my friend," I said. "I honestly don't believe you're serious when you say that. A denial of God means that you're despoiling and despising human personality. You are robbing man of his towering spiritual beliefs, beliefs that function for the enrichment of the whole community. You are injuring your own self, your word and thought and outlook! Surely you are big enough to see that Christianity seeks a supreme, happy world state, based on man's free choice, on his acceptance of moral and spiritual values. Jesus came to proclaim God as universal Father and man His son, committed to follow the path of peace, love and good will on earth. In that world-wide brotherhood there is no violence, torture, imprisonment, slavery. Men and women are not treated as robots as totalitarian systems seek to treat them. Christianity offers them the sacred rights of children of God, endowed with spiritual capacities because they are made in the image of God. With your intelligence surely you ought to see that compared with Christianity, materialism is a very poor alternative with its absolute, soulless theory that man is just a means, that the end, the important end, is the state."

He gave me a baleful look.

"Oh, what's the good of talking?" he said defiantly. "What you say, or a lot of it, is all bunk. You and your God! I tell you, I don't believe in God. Let's be sensible and not waste time on this ridiculous religious tomfoolery. If there is such a God as you say, why didn't He make a better show of things? Why has He given me a bad deal? Tell me that?"

So he wanted a God Who would grant him favours, give him a safe and easy passage through life! How like so many others? "If disappointment and ordeal dog my life I will not believe in Him!" I glanced at his set face and hostile eyes.

"Jim," I said feelingly, "I'm not going to push God down your throat. I'm sure He'll catch up with you one day. I wouldn't be a bit surprised if already He's paid you a visit, left His visiting card with you. Look, don't let's go on arguing. We can do that till the cows come home. You say you want a better world. So do I. I believe that that better world will come only when we both realise that men's hearts have got to be changed by spiritual means, not material ones. It isn't force or tyranny or an all-powerful material state that's going to bring in that better world.

It's only through an acknowledgement of a Power outside the material world that will do it. Please don't try to rob men and women of their beautiful faith in the Living and Eternal God. As I see it, outside of God, human life can develop into nothing more than a dry rot, a creeping palsy."

We talked to a very late hour. Our conversation was very often disturbed by the heavy footsteps of derelict men in the passage-way seeking a mission bed for the night. Before we parted I noticed a distinct change in my companion. His attitude of enmity and truculence towards me altered perceptibly. His repugnant exhibition of cynicism and churlishness gave way to a friendly spirit of reason and cordiality. He asked to see me again. Gripping my hand firmly as he left, his face puckered into a slight smile.

"Life has its funny side, hasn't it," he said. "Fancy me talking to a Bible puncher about religion! What would my comrades say?"

He smiled again, this time more broadly as I answered him.

"Tell your comrades you've been talking about the highest, the best things in life. Tell them you're not going to miss the true purpose of life, the best joys that life can afford. Tell them, Jim, that you're going to see to it that your Saviour Jesus Christ will not be disappointed in you."

On one of his further visits he told me something of his past life. He grew up in a broken home, his father having left his mother in Brisbane where he was born. Mother had to go out to work to keep her young family, returning home in the evening frequently exhausted and fretful because of her long hours charring in private houses. Concerned increasingly about her sick condition, Jim developed a spirit of antagonism toward those who lived in big houses and owned expensive cars. In his teen-age years he mixed with some older men who told him that the labouring classes were having a bad social and economic deal, that a world revolution was needed and that the only political people likely to bring it about were those who belonged to their extreme group. He joined it, took classes in their particular theories, and sought to understand dialectical materialism. God never came into his thought; Jesus Christ was a myth. He sold atheistic literature, became a public speaker and a recognised leader of the city freethinkers. Moving to Sydney, he visited sundry open-air spaces where public debates were allowed, strenuously advocated his political faith, whipping up support for his longed-for workers' revolution.

My preaching and lecture engagements eventually took me to New Zealand for a busy two months. On my return I wrote to Jim inviting him once again to visit me. I heard nothing for several days. Then I was summoned to the telephone to hear his agonised voice pleading for me to go to him.

"I'm in hell!" he shouted, "in hell!"

I found him in a small, repulsive room over a café in the dock area. The whole neighbourhood seemed to cringe from public gaze as if ashamed of its dirt and destitution. Jim sat before a smouldering fire. The few coals in the grate seemed to cling together for warmth. His feet rested on an old sack which was the only floor covering in the room. His forehead was badly gashed and his right foot and ankle tightly bandaged. He told me that he had been having a drunken spell and had got mixed up with a fighting gang. He was contrite and admitted that he was in an awful shape, both in body and mind.

"Makes you think!" he said sadly, "hiding away here.

Hiding even from myself. I've got a bed, such as it is and an apology of a room. I've also got pain, pain in my thought, pain in my loneliness. Good God, so I've come to this! What's going to be the end of it?"

He went on to tell me that his landlord was indifferent to his suffering, only allowing him to use his phone to ring me. Also that not one of his party friends had been to see him, although he had been confined to his room for over two weeks.

"I had to go to hospital to have my leg attended to," he went on. "One of the orderlies recognised me. 'You're the chap who spouts on atheism up on the green, aren't you?' he said. 'Don't seem to have done you much good, eh? Look at you! A bit knocked about! Give it up, old digger, and go in for something that'll bring you more credit.' Loafing here day after day, seeing nobody, only a girl who brings me a little food from the shop, I've been thinking hard about what that codger said. I tell you, I'm in the hell of a mess. My body aches, my leg troubles me and worst of all, I'm all fouled up in my mind. You know, I'm not so sure now whether I'm on the right lines after all. I mean, my political lines."

This last remark of his sent a quickening thrill of hope through my being. I felt very sorry for him. The marks of grievous suffering were deeply etched in his furrowed cheeks. His eyes were heavy with sadness. Nevertheless, watching him sympathetically, I was glad that he had come to the road where, looking back, he could see that his materialistic creed had brought him very little pride or satisfaction. My heart cried silently for grace and wisdom from above to help my struggling, distressed companion. I laid my hand gently on his arm.

"Jim, old man," I said quietly, "I'm glad I'm a Christian because I feel I have something of great value to say to you.

You've been thinking hard you say. Well, Christianity is good for one's thought. It says, your mind gives back to you only what you put into it. 'As a man thinketh in his heart, so is he.' Your thinking has troubled you. Why not shift from despondent negative thoughts to enlivening positive ones! For instance, listen to this. 'God has not given us the spirit of fear, but of power and love and of a sound mind.' Here's another. 'The things which are impossible with men are possible with God.' And this—'I can do all things through Christ which strengtheneth me.' Those are not only words, you know. They're power—distilled power. Will you allow me to say this to you. I do want to help you. I speak to you as a friend. Those texts I quoted were from the Bible. Because they're in the Bible, please don't ridicule them. The Bible is a store-house of the highest wisdom. It contains powerful, uplifting thoughts that directly apply to you. Why not fill your mind with them? Millions of people do. I know there's some queer folk who call themselves Christians. But they're not all queer. Some of the brainiest, outstanding men of character in our midst are Christians. You know that. Fill your mind with these scriptural statements. Let them seep deep down in your consciousness. Then your mind will give back to you strong, positive, glowing thoughts to oppose your negative ones. Why not try it? I'll give you a Bible."

A wan smile creased his face.

"A Bible! Christian thoughts! You asking me to try out religion? Me, a dyed-in-the-wool atheist! A recognised antagonist of Christianity! Bearded in my own den! And yet, somehow I believe you may have something. Maybe, if I hadn't advocated positive godlessness so strongly, I wouldn't have been in this hole."

He spoke wistfully, hung his head down and emitted a slight moan.

"I'm quite sure you wouldn't," I replied. "Atheism is destructive. I can hardly imagine it filling a man's soul with unutterable peace. Let me say another mouthful and a true one, Jim. You are miserable. I'm quite sure you will never know complete happiness, peace and victory until you know Jesus Christ as your Saviour and Friend."

Time passed rapidly as we talked together. His attitude was friendly and co-operative. He showed himself ready, almost anxious to hear what I had to say. His agnostic belief had whipped him to sadness and defeat. I visited him twice more in his dismal room and each time, tactfully I presented the claims of my Lord on his life. On the second occasion I asked him if he minded my praying and reading the Bible to him. Rather than objecting he said he would be glad if I would. The story of the leper in Matthew's Gospel seemed to suit the condition of us both.

" 'And there came a leper to Him saying, "Lord, if Thou wilt, Thou canst make me clean." And Jesus put forth His hand saying, "I will, be thou clean." Immediately, his leprosy was cleansed.'

"Jim," I continued, "my brief is this. I don't bring you another -ism but I do bring you the Person of Jesus Christ. You need a personal Saviour, Someone directly interested in you. Right now you can turn your back on your old life and receive by faith the new life He has for you. That's vitally and gloriously true. You can hold fellowship with God through Jesus Christ. You can enter into partnership with Him, be welcomed into His loving family. I've seen that happen to many 'lepers'—bad men, sad men, men of unclean lips and lives. I've seen hundreds of freed and happy men thank God for regenerating power that has caused them to live a joyous, Christ-dedicated existence. His character, His life rings true. Don't forget, He has trod your earthly road—and mine. You may follow Him through all your pain and perplexity. Read about Him in this New Testament. This is not a book of rubbish. It contains the highest, holiest truth that both of us can ever face up to. Look! He touches people with hands of healing. He speaks to them and peace comes into their hearts. He makes the blind to see, the lame to walk, the foulest to be made clean. He loves folk of all types and conditions with a strong, tender love. He died at thirty-three still loving them. Man, what great and vital news! He came to forgive and deliver you from your sins, to give you inward peace that nothing can break. He can put you on top of life instead of underneath it. What's the saying? 'He is able to save to the uttermost them that come unto God through Him.' What about it, Jim? Jesus, your Saviour, is waiting for your decision. Don't refuse Him. Please obey Him, follow Him at all costs."

I felt that I had spoken too long but he gave me such concentrated attention that it was easy to talk to him. He asked for time to consider what I had said and admitted that he was not only interested but challenged. We arranged to meet in my room as soon as he was able to get out.

A week passed, then I got a ring saying he was coming round to see me. When he entered my mission room, one quick glance showed that a regenerating work of Christian grace had gone on in his heart since I left him. His eyes shone with evident pleasure at our renewed meeting. His hand grip was firm. He spoke in a happy, stimulating voice. The bruise had healed on his forehead and the bandage was off his foot. His face lit up with inner victory. Quickly he seated himself, nodded to me and began:

"You'll be glad to know that I've told Christ I'm on His side from now on. I made my stand the other night. I've

c

been thinking seriously about Christianity since we met, and I see now it's for me. Christ wants me to be His disciple so I've said all right, I'm your man. I asked myself, is there any other way of living which is better than what I've gone in for, that is for many years. I own to having been a rotter. I've drunk many a pub almost dry; I've sworn and whored and fought. I've denounced Christianity and Christians day in and day out for umpteen years. What good has it done me? A one-roomed home, no real friends, no money and a sick mind and soul. Thinking it over constantly because of the rotten condition I was in, I knew there was something different, something better. So I thought hard, considered what you had said to me and what I knew Christianity stood for and made my decision. I got out of bed on Tuesday night, knelt down by its side and said this—'Dear Jesus Christ, I will follow you. Please forgive me for my sinful past. I'm turning my back on everything but you.' Just that!"

He stopped suddenly and smiled across at me. I considered for a moment what he had said, then involuntarily found myself exclaiming—"Amen."

In the weeks that followed, while I was in Australia, Jim became a mighty power for good in Christian assemblies and among his former rationalist associates. He joined a Witnessing Fellowship in the city and travelled about holding services. It was a glad day when I received this heartening letter from him:

"Christ is my all in all. I must follow Him and witness for Him. He shall have my best. I will try and build the real new universe with His help. I know He has the Key that all the world is seeking. He does things, He changes things. He has changed me. I'm doing a little speaking for Him. I've been reading about those missionaries who lost their lives in the Amazon jungle. I'm thinking of offering myself to the South American Mission. I'd love to go and live with those tribes who don't get much chance to hear the Gospel. Please pray for me. In His glad service.

Jim."

Chapter 5

JESUS SAID: "ABIDE IN MY LOVE."

I THEN found myself in New Zealand.

The People's Mission in Auckland is a bright spiritual lighthouse in the city. Its zealous superintendent, Mr. Keith Rimmer, is a recognised religious giant throughout the dominion. Oftentimes, at his invitation, I preached in his mission and shared fellowship with his good people, enthusiastic in their evangelical life and witness.

A very large class of church-going folk have a mistaken idea that those who go to missions are typical gutter mouchers, such as can only be found during the week lounging in cheap lodging houses or living in slum quarters. This is certainly not so. In our own country as well as all over the world, in undenominational evangelical missions I have found doctors, lawyers, editors, educated men in almost every walk of life, who have found in those mission halls what they could not find in the denominational orthodox churches: wholesome spiritual meat for their souls. Frequently, weary in mind, body and soul, they have gone to their churches ardently desiring a tonic religious meal, only to be fobbed off with a measly insipid presentation of one that brought on an acute attack of mental and spiritual indigestion.

Who wants to hear an insipid address about a musty theological dogma? In this demanding and difficult world in which we live, all of us who use our brains to think of the serious issues of life, and their relationship to human personality, wish to know how to become more than conquerors over every trial that confronts us. We want to hear the Eternal constant truth that makes sense of life, that reveals it as a grand and superb adventure, the thrilling truth that Christ Jesus loved us so much that He died for us, that even today He rescues us from our lowest self and lifts us into the intimacy of His enduring companionship.

That is the essence of the Gospel preached in *The People's Mission* and in most of the other missions I have been proud to be associated with, at home and abroad.

It was after one of my services in the Auckland Mission that at the door I shook hands with a well-dressed man who waited behind for a few minutes to see me. He was tall and slim, grey-haired, clean shaven, with blue eyes that looked sad behind rimless glasses. I judged him to be in his early sixties. He gave me a faint smile and stepped back from the door, away from people who were having a friendly word.

"I enjoyed the service," he said quietly, in a soft cultured voice. "It's quite a long time since I was in a church, but I saw in the local press that you were here; and knowing you in England, I thought I would come and hear you. I'm from the old country too, and if you're interested I could say a little that would probably surprise you. If you're too busy to see me, just say the word and I'll be on my way."

In my long ministry I have tried hard not to appear disinterested in total strangers who wanted to take up my time in telling me about themselves and their particular concerns and pressing problems. I have endeavoured to suffer fools gladly, to give heed to sorrowful tales, both genuine and counterfeit. Often I have listened to hard-luck stories, given loans which were never repaid and been outrageously lied to and wilfully deceived. In my own home hostel I have had men who were finely skilled in telling a tale that would move the hardest of hearts. Yet not all have been scamps who have come to me soliciting alms and friendship. Gladly I testify that in my ministry among those unfortunate enough to enter the ranks of the 'down-and-outs' I have found some who at the last day, because of their strongly-held Christian faith and steadfast courage in the midst of much that was grievous and harassing, will be found an honoured place in the Father's Home. I nodded affably at my companion.

"Of course I'm interested," I replied with a smile of friendship. "So you too are from England. I've met many of my own countrymen over here. Go ahead and tell me what you're doing in Auckland."

For answer, he gave me a serious look as if undecided whether or not to share his confidences with me. Then his face creased into an expression of approval. From an inner coat pocket he brought out a buckskin wallet and handed me his name-card. It was a hyphenated name and as a business address gave a well-known insurance firm in the city. My companion was its local manager. As he handed me the card I detected a faint smell of alcohol.

"Look," he said, pleasantly, "have you a spare half-hour within the next few days? I don't want to talk here. I'd like to invite you to my home. We can get together better there. It's more private. Come and have a cup of coffee with me. Let me say, by the way, I don't want to urge you to take out an insurance policy. Nothing of that kind. I'd just like to have a chat. I don't think you'll waste your time. Maybe you'll find we have a little in common, and—well, you may do me some good."

He stopped abruptly, took the card from me and wrote another address on the back of it.

"That's my private address. Just outside the city. Give me a ring when you're free to come and I'll be glad to see you." He gripped my hand firmly, gathered up a bowler hat and gloves and swiftly left the mission.

An attractive village outside Auckland is mostly inhabited by city workers in good commercial positions and its houses are chiefly those of the middle-class type. One evening, soon after our first meeting, I found my acquaintance in a very pleasant dwelling, situated in a third of an acre of ground. Answering my doorbell ring he greeted me with a friendly smile and escorted me to a very well-furnished room. A woman he introduced as his housekeeper brought in coffee and biscuits and quickly departed. We talked a few pleasantries about the country and the purpose of my visit to it. Then, settling himself comfortably in his armchair, he gave me an intent gaze and spoke very quietly and earnestly.

"I'm going to ask you to respect my confidence," he said, "that is, not to say anything about me while you're in Auckland, or, if you don't mind, while you're in this part of the country. You have my full permission to make reference to me by word or in writing after you've left New Zealand if you think any good purpose can come of it. If you do, please don't use my surname. Call me Bob. That'll do. The fact is that a few years ago, that is, before the last war, our names were in the same ministerial year book. I'm an ex-Free Church minister, one of many who have left the ministry. Why did I leave it? That's a long story but it wasn't on doctrinal grounds. In a sentence, it was because I couldn't stand it any longer, couldn't stand the church set-up, the sheer paltriness of many of the people I had to mix with and the everlasting trivial meetings that I was expected to attend. Above all, I couldn't stand the exhausting poverty that just took all the life out of me. So I quit. I don't want you to think that because I left the Church I've gone on the downward path, that I'm now a despicable pagan, a shameful worldling. That just isn't true. I like my drink and I'm not above doing a few other things that don't bring me entire satisfaction. But I've got my pride and I've still got my high valuation of things, both moral and spiritual. Having been brought up in the Church and been a parson for a few years, I admit, I'm still troubled by the old insistent call. Oh yes, like Joan of Arc, I sometimes hear heavenly voices. D'you know, I heard Billy Graham in the open air here and found myself admiring him for much he said. But of course he's a free-lance and doesn't have the church worries that attend many parsons. I'm not boring you, am I?"

"Indeed you're not," I answered eagerly. "I'm intensely interested and glad you asked me round. Go ahead!"

He poured me out another cup of coffee, furrowed his brow and continued his story. It was evident that he was glad to unburden himself of thoughts and feelings that chafed his mind, happy to talk to one who had travelled his ministerial road, who understood fully his lot when he was a pastoral shepherd.

He proceeded to tell me that in his short ministerial career he had had three churches. He had gone to them full of godly enthusiasm, keenly anxious to win people to Jesus Christ. He had worked hard, stimulated the interest of the public in his services by relating the problems of the day to the Christian Gospel, originated men's forums and Bible schools and put each of the churches decisively on the religious as well as the local town map. The weekly collections had been doubled and in one case trebled. Yet not from one of the churches had he received a single penny increase on his yearly stipend. He told me that when he was first ordained to the Christian ministry his yearly income was £160. His lodgings cost him nearly £3 weekly. When he asked his church secretary, a man whom it was well known had an excellent financial position, if the church could give him another £10 a year, he was sanctimoniously warned against having "an inordinate love of money" and his request for this small financial rise icily refused.

His poignant story was painfully disturbing and familiar to me. How often have I heard it in my travels up and down the country from present-day ministers and from those who have left the ministry! Let us be strictly honest with ourselves. Why wonder that in the Free Churches especially there are dozens of vacant pastorates; that among many still serving pastors there is a positive mood of restlessness, dissatisfaction and frustration; that young men who might revitalise organised religion are turning their talents to science, industry and education! For far too long many Nonconformist churches have callously imposed the heavy strain of poverty on men who have obeyed the call of God to preach the Gospel and care for His people. As employers they are among the worst in the country when it comes to paying their employees a living wage.

Most ministers have sat in church meetings companioned by business men in good financial situations, in receipt of regular bonuses and rises, and heard them boringly talk about many trivial subjects. It is regrettably true to say that very, very few of these ministers have heard their comfortably-placed deacons suggest a slight increase in the ministerial stipend despite the fact that year after year the church has been progressively flourishing.

The cause of this aggravating, injurious trouble is, I am sure, two-fold. One, the very low regard in which the impoverished minister is far too often held by regular church goers. How can the Christian Church hope to convince the world that it has a message of salvation when it continues to employ cheap ministerial labour? There is something appallingly wrong with any church which pays its minister, who has had precisely as long an educational training as a doctor and a solicitor, who usually possesses intellectual gifts of a high order, less than a dustman or a twenty-year-old bus conductress.

The second, and much bigger cause of the calamity which hinders the spread of the Gospel and the spiritual progress of the Church, is that there are simply not enough truly consecrated Christians *in* the Church. If only our churches were filled with people who had Christ at the centre and circumference of their lives, would not the pressing financial problems both of the church and the minister be quickly solved? I am persuaded that they soon would be. With the New Testament open before them and the picture of Christ plainly within their view, their consciences would not allow them to live on a very low level, to reveal to the world the glaring vices of selfishness, unkindness as well as meanness towards others.

These thoughts passed through my mind as I listened sympathetically to my companion's recriminations against the Church and the Christian ministry. What he felt was a hard deal he had had from the Church had made him very bitter and antagonistic. As he spoke his eyes grew hard, his face was furrowed with inner pain and his manner became increasingly restless. Suddenly he rose to his feet, paced to and fro for a moment, then came to a halt before me. He spoke slowly and with great deliberation as though each word were costing him a big effort.

"Do you realise, Frank—you don't mind my calling you Frank, do you?—some of our churches tend to drive the minister to the devil by their sheer callousness regarding his well-being and their stinginess to him! Do you know that when my wife was seriously ill, an illness from which she eventually died, not one of the officers of the church I had then took the trouble to call at my house to see how she was! What do you think of that? Don't forget, I was their minister. As long as I turned up on the Sunday and gave them two soothing messages—that's all they cared. Religion eh? How can you expect the Church to make progress if you have in it people of that frigid, uncaring type? Why is it that the vast majority of parsons' sons never enter the ministry? You know the reason. They see what their own father had to go through with some of his church members. I'm no snob. God forbid! But in my own ministry I saw that the Church was so weak in man power that we simply couldn't find suitable folk to put into office. So just anybody was put in, men and women, with no talents nor education, nor even Christ converted people. Often I just ached to have someone among my officers to pray with me, to say a kindly word about my work among them. But no. They couldn't do it. Like dozens of other parsons, I came to feel intellectually and spiritually lonely and often wondered whether my long, exacting struggle to fit myself for the ministry, five years' hard grind in college, was really worth it. Man, if I hadn't got out I'd have had a nervous breakdown."

He walked quickly to his chair and sat down heavily. A feeling of immense relief flooded my mind as he did so. I was glad when he ceased to fulminate against the Church, not because it was untrue what he said but because, unhappily, I knew it was only too true and the truth saddened me.

In my open-air work, dealing with Christians and antagonists to the Christian faith, how often had I heard the charge that some churches were like refrigerators, that the glory of God had departed from them, that some people stayed away not because they were irreligious but because their church so often seemed to have lower values than their own.

Many years ago in Chicago I talked to Billy Sunday, the famous American ex-baseball player, and then superintendent of the famous Pacific Garden Mission in which he was converted.

"I've come across churches," he said, "that were so cold that I fully expected to see icicles hanging from the lights and sidesmen taking up the collection on skates. I've frequently found more fellowship among my golfing associates than I have among many church members. The trouble with our churches, my boy, is that too many office bearers in it are entire strangers to Christ. How can any pastor do his proper job, that of winning men and women to their Lord and Saviour, when much of his devoted labour is consumed in raising money and he has to mix with those on Sunday who have little care for the spiritual business of the Church! Can't be done!"

I have often wondered what kind of a welcome would many of our churches give to a prostitute who wandered in from the street or to the convict who had just come out of prison. The likely and tragic truth is that the Church is the last place to which these human casualties would turn.

I looked across at my companion with a pitying eye. In the privacy of that very comfortable room I saw a human mind in grievous anguish. Wearily he sat in his chair as if the recital of his Church complaint had sorely taxed his mental and physical strength. The corroding acid of his feeling against Christian people and Christian organisations had burnt deeply into his soul. I felt that if my visit was going to be worth while I must try to change the subject and lead him to consider more satisfying issues.

"Bob," I said softly, "I'm your guest and I'm glad to be here and to share in your heart thoughts and emotions. You know, I do understand and sympathise with much you have said. I do whole-heartedly agree that there is a lot that is seriously wrong with the Christian Church, that many of its ministers, finding themselves preaching to the same handful of mind-and-soul impoverished folk week after week, feel themselves in a losing position. I know all that. I know that for numerous parsons, as the Church gets weaker and weaker, the ministry can be real heart and life travail. I've had some of it myself. I'd like you to know that. In common with others I, too, have had my mental and spiritual agonies regarding some church happenings and some church people. But look! Is this sort of controversy and criticism going to help you? We can go on criticising the Church till the cows come home. Much is wrong with it you say, and I agree. The Church is made up of human personalities. Haven't we an urgent job to try to do something with them? What you have been talking about is cold, deadening Churchianity. What about dynamic, pulsing Christianity? What about Christ? Isn't He bigger than the Church, than all the churches? When you became a Christian was it because of the Church or because of Jesus? Please, don't revel in mere church controversy. Don't you think that our supreme job is to stress the Christian faith that unites and heals, to rejoice in the liberty wherewith Christ has made us free and to welcome all of any class or colour who readily turn to the Saviour Who saves and redeems? I do. Can I go on?"

A pleasant smile crept round the corners of his mouth and up into his face. He nodded. "Yes do," he replied.

"Of course, I realise you're talking common sense. Maybe I've become over-critical of the Church since I left it, and I haven't had a chat of this kind for quite a time. Yes, go on. It's for the good of my soul, I know."

"Bob," I resumed, "I wish we could turn the Church into a Life-Changing Agency, its members rallying to aid the minister in season and out of season, ready and capable to lead any lost prodigals, both within and outside the Church, to the foot of the Cross. What a day that would be if we could only bring it about! Say all church members increasingly on their knees, looking up into the Face of Christ, vowing to give Him the full, unstinted service of their lives. If only, if only that mighty miracle could take place don't you think that all our problems that matter, ministerial, financial, spiritual, would be happily solved? Of course they would. Don't forget, you and I are part of the Church. If we are indifferent about answering God's calls on us, then the Church is bound to suffer and our own spiritual life begins to weaken."

I paused to see whether my words were having any effect on my companion. He was reclining comfortably in his chair, contentedly smoking a cigarette and watching me keenly all the time. I felt that his mood was encouragingly co-operative, so continued.

"Our big trouble, Bob, is that for many of us Jesus Christ is not real enough. We haven't a living Lord leaping to claim our loyalty, love and service. How can we give Him consistent discipleship both in the Church and outside of it if we refuse to receive what He has to give us? As I see it, not until we are prepared to receive God's love through Jesus can we have a self worth giving. We are left with a stale, deadly apology of the Christian Gospel that numbers us with so many of our moribund, sub-Christian congregations. Don't you agree?"

He stubbed out his cigarette and shifted uneasily from side to side. I thought I noticed a slight flush creeping into his cheeks and a mistiness appear in his eyes.

"For some years," he said gently, "I've been like a cork on life's sea, just tossed about anyhow. I admit that. I've had no spiritual authority. Simply lost it. I could see no light ahead. But listening to you I do now see a glimmer of it."

Quickly I butted in.

"The light is in your own heart, Bob. Please don't let it go out. Keep it burning, the light of your love for Christ. You remember what Jesus said to Peter. 'Simon, I have prayed that thy faith fail not.'"

"Sometimes sitting here alone," he replied, "I look back on the days of my conversion. How happy I was! How anxious to save souls for Him! And then—oh well, let that pass. I confess that occasionally I get the old longing to be now what I used to be. You know, out and out for Him, in charge of some little church working side by side with God, the greatest Power in the universe. That gives me renewed hope and purpose. Then I do nothing about it."

He inbreathed deeply and cupped his chin in his left hand. His frank and tender word warmed my heart. I felt that although he had been out of the Church for some years a personal devotion to Christ was welling within him again, that the Presence of his Lord was not very far from him. I was determined before I left the house to seek to win his surrender to God, to urge him to base his life on the standards of His Son and get him to work for the furtherance of His kingdom on earth.

"My dear Bob," I said, "I do appreciate your confidence in me, giving me the benefit of some of your deepest thoughts. You know, you can get a glorious future out of yesterday's past. Why don't you once again reconsecrate yourself to Christ? Think of Him passing on the stage of human history, illuminating life with new beauty, sacredness and courage. Recall what you know about Him, how men and women found new faith in themselves because He loved and trusted them. Wastrels, harlots, down-and-outs entered a new life of purity, strength and truth because He became their beloved Friend. How about you? Why not find release in Him and great joy again in witnessing earnestly for His cause? We simply mustn't release Barabbas and crucify Christ. What about it?"

It was midnight before we broke off our very profitable conversation. I asked him before leaving if he minded my having a word of prayer. Gladly he assented and I prayed that we both might know the solid delight of serving our common Master and Lord, experience the forgiveness of our many sins, clear the way for His ministry in our lives and allow us to help share His miracles among those with whom we lived. He drove me back to the city, saying very little, yet, I felt, thinking very much. It was arranged that I should see him again the following week. Two days later I received an unexpected yet welcome letter that sent a thrill through my being and caused me to ejaculate a fervent "Thank God!" Twice over I read the letter.

"My dear Frank, I feel I must say thank you for your visit to me on Tuesday evening and for what you said. When I returned home after leaving you I felt no desire to sleep, so I put on my dressing gown and went downstairs. In my chair I thought of our conversation and looked back on my past. I saw myself as a broken spiritual reed, how I had run away from my proper job, that of preaching the Gospel. Once more, the inward conflict which has troubled me for some years was renewed. I felt very unhappy and dissatisfied and realised that I couldn't go on with the old life. Not, as I told you, that I have been a big sinner but I recognised full well that I have fallen very short of the high calling that once I placed before me. I had to do something about it in order to experience again real happiness and peace of mind. So I made the great decision last night. The barriers of caddishness and self-love went down and on my knees I surrendered myself afresh to Jesus Christ. I feel that, with God's help, I have come back from the dark places of the soul and once more can walk and act with dignity—spiritual dignity. Now I am truly relieved, free. A great load is off my heart. I want now to live for Him, yes, and to die for Him. When you come, please let us have Holy Communion together. I feel I would like that.

"Your sincere friend and brother in Christ,

Bob."

I recall vividly the simple and memorable scene. The pleasant room, a small table covered by a lily-white table-cloth. On it the shining paten containing three tiny cubes of bread. Also three individual communion cups partly filled with sacramental wine. Two eager, newly-consecrated people, Bob and his housekeeper, sitting in front of me.

"The Lord God is a sun and shield. The Lord will give grace and glory. No good thing will He withhold from them that walk uprightly."

"Trust in the Lord and do good. So shalt thou dwell in the land and verily thou shalt be fed."

Let Thy Blood in mercy poured,
Let Thy gracious Body broken,
Be to me, O gracious Lord,
Of Thy boundless love the token.
Thou didst give Thyself for me,
Now I give myself to Thee.

"Ye who do truly and earnestly repent you of your sins and are in love and charity with your neighbours and intend to lead a new life, following the commandments of God and walking from henceforth in His holy ways——"

In my remaining weeks in New Zealand I saw a complete transformation in the mind and heart and soul of my friend Bob. He lived the simple, exciting life of a true disciple of his beloved Lord Jesus Christ. When I went to say goodbye to him, appealing happiness and contentment was reflected in his whole personality.

"You will be glad to know," he said with enthusiasm, "that I've started my own Bible class here on Sunday afternoons, that I've joined the Presbyterian Church in the city and that I'm looking round for some undenominational mission to superintend. I'd love to be back in the work again. I know now more about Christ's unfailing power to save sinners to the uttermost and am very anxious to pass on the good news of His saving power to others. What has happened to me—this spiritual rebirth—is so momentous that I feel it's the most important thing I know of to talk about. I literally hunger to tell others about One Who loves them through life and through death. When I was ordained we sang that lovely old hymn known by most Christians. I'm going to make it my own daily, consecration prayer.

> *Moment by moment I'm kept in His love.*
> *Moment by moment I've life from above.*
> *Looking to Jesus till glory doth shine,*
> *Moment by moment, O Lord I am Thine."*

Chapter 6

JESUS SAID: "FOLLOW ME!"

WHEN I was a Summer preacher in the town of Northampton, Massachusetts in recent years, I often ministered in the church made famous by the fiery and eloquent Rev. Jonathan Edwards. During his very successful ministry, Edwards held a Question Night, during which his church members plied him with various Biblical questions. Most of these questions he wrote down in a notebook. How trivial and unimportant the majority of them read today! "Who were the sons of Noah?" "Who built the city of Samaria?" "How many altars were in use in the Tabernacle?" "What do you know about Shem?"

I thought about Edwards and his many Bible questioners as I sat in my bedroom in "The Bridge", Wellington, New Zealand, facing two keen-minded men anxious to improve their religious knowledge and to eradicate from their minds many lurking theological doubts.

"The Bridge" is a well-known, highly-favoured institution owned by the Salvation Army and devoted exclusively to their priceless and commendable Alcoholics Anonymous ministry. I had been invited to the city of Wellington by Colonel Bramwell Cook, Chief Secretary of the Salvation Army throughout New Zealand. Col. Cook, a man of deep spiritual experience, an able preacher and administrator, is also an outstanding, highly qualified surgeon. "The Bridge" is aptly named because those fortunate enough to enter it are shown the way that leads from alcoholic poisoning to healthy sobriety, from life's dismal failure to ennobling success, from Satanic slavery to freedom and victory in and through the dynamic power of the Saviour Christ.

My two companions were temporary residents and guests of the Salvation Army at "The Bridge". They were shamed, sorrowful ex-alcoholics. Sid was an accountant, and had audited the books of large city firms for a number of years. He had gradually degenerated into a bottle slave and in consequence had upset his home and bankrupted his business life. Len had been a builder. Fierce competition had beaten him in his trade. As a result he sought to drown his sorrows in the whisky flask and inevitably found himself within a few years a hardened, weak-willed drunk and derelict. Because of the compassionate love they had received from Salvation Army officials, the mental and spiritual atmosphere that enclosed them and the Christian teaching they freely and helpfully received from those in whose charge they were committed, both men were eager to ply me with questions at the close of my first meeting with a group of ex-alcoholic victims at "The Bridge". I singled them out as earnest seekers after truth, wholeheartedly anxious to establish their future goings in the ways of respectability. But they felt their appalling ignorance of the Christian faith and desired to know more about its content and purpose. Hence the meeting in my bedroom, the first of several during my series of engagements in the city. For two hours, questions and answers were bandied to and fro. They went something like this. I was "Frank".

Sid: "I'm sure I speak for Len when I say that it's very good of you to meet us in this way. The fact is that we're both in need of instruction in regard to Christian teaching.

You know, Christian belief and what the Church teaches. We feel we've learned our lesson and would like to know what makes a Christian; what does the Salvation Army mean when it talks about blood and fire?"

Frank: "That goes for you too, Len?"

Len: "Oh yes! I'm with Sid. I've heard the arguments from atheists against Christianity. Can you tell us more about God, prove Him to be?"

Frank: "Right! Let's start there. First. It is easier to ask some questions than to answer them. Also, it depends on what some people mean when they ask for 'proof'. It's not simple, is it, to prove a mother's love for her child. If I could answer every question regarding the Christian faith then I'd very soon cease to be human. I'd be in the nature of a small god myself, finding little difficulty in running the world rather than in trying to explain it. Always remember too, that mere head knowledge is not enough, especially concerning matters of the Christian faith. Heart life counts tremendously here. The heart can often answer questions when all argument is of little avail. But I'm going to add this. The Christian faith has been with us for nigh two thousand years. It has been tested by the reason of countless millions and tried out in their lives daily and successfully. Any sincere and serious minded person can intelligently put his or her trust in it. One of my vagabond friends got converted. At an open-air meeting, he gave his religious testimony. A heckler shouted to him, 'You're out of your depth, Bill!' 'Maybe,' replied Bill, 'but I can swim.' Doesn't that mean that Christian truth is not a prerogative of the clever or learned. 'The secret of the Lord is with them that fear Him.' Now Len, you ask about God?"

Len: "That's it! I'd really like to make use of a few points in argument in His favour when I'm challenged."

Frank: "We get most of our thoughts, certainly our best thoughts, about Him from the Bible. Think of God as a spiritual personal Being. He is generally acknowledged as the Supreme Power behind the universe and from Whom the universe had its origin. Start there! God is the world's Designer, the Supreme Intelligence behind the order, wisdom and beauty found in the world. He is the great Lover of the human race. He is generous and compassionate and kind in thought and purpose. In all discussion about God, don't forget, we must always primarily take account of Jesus for He is God in the human scene. But remember God is Spirit, Infinite and therefore beyond full human conception."

Len: "What about the atheist? I mean if there's no God as he keeps on saying, then Christians are up a gum tree, aren't they? They're wasting their time."

Frank: "Quite right, Len. You know, I've the feeling that when an atheist shouts himself hoarse yelling—'There is no God' he has a sneaking fear that God may be listening to him. If no God, why take Him into consideration? These great Christian works; these superb painters with their Christian pictures; these amazing builders and architects with their beautiful churches and cathedrals; these sculptors expressing their ennobling piety in statues of saints and prophets of old. In fact, all Christian workers. Well, they've all been misled. Their brains have been used in a foolish cause. If no God, all Christians today must be misled. The sooner we turn our glorious churches into garages or Bingo institutions and tell the Salvation Army to cease its religious propaganda, stop its bands from playing 'Rescue the perishing, care for the dying', close down organisations like Alcoholic Anonymous and Christian Endeavour Societies, the better. The atheist's creed is the creed of unwisdom, despair and hopelessness.

Accept it and you'll soon run into personal gloom and world chaos."

Len: "I must try to remember some of those points. I believe that the Christian Church as well as the Salvation Army has got something. I've played the fool for years. So has Sid. I've done so because I've had no power to live a creative life. I've just gone on in a ceaseless round of boozing and selfishness. There seemed nothing else worth living for. Many times I felt myself just lost. Then all at once my mind seemed to open and I saw that I could live a better and happier life, with a lot of decency and purpose in it if I tried to live according to the Christian standard of truth and goodness. Let the atheist call me a simpleton if he likes. All I know is that I'm gradually getting out of the clutches of the drink habit because I feel that a new inner power is making me stronger. I believe that's God getting inside me. I'm sure of it. I'd rather accept the Christian belief than side with the atheist with his contention that religion is 'dope'."

Frank: "Well spoken, Len! As I see it, the atheist with his 'dope' ridicule of Christianity comes very near to taking all meaning out of life. He deprives the universe of any spiritual standard of goodness and beauty. He turns his back on One Who would be his greatest Friend, Jesus Christ; he throws out man's deep-seated belief in immortality; he denies his own highest and noblest instincts. That's not good enough. Believe me, Christians have a strong case for Christianity and they are able to state it positively, defend and commend it. The Christian faith fully answers the constant questionings of mind and soul and offers the final and complete truth about human existence. If we're going to say that the universe as well as life came into being with no thought or design, just in a chancy, haphazard way, then that assertion and standpoint makes complete nonsense of life as we see it to be, life in all its majesty, purpose and power."

Sid: "This is a refreshing discussion to me, you know. I mean, it encourages me in my Christian search. I feel I'm learning a good deal. I'm beginning to see that with a right view of God a man can build up a faith in himself and in the world."

Frank: "Quite right! Let's finish this line of thought by saying that we live in a world that has all the evidence of Divine Creation. We Christians strongly believe that the kindly Power behind creation is the true Reality. We also affirm that we can know that Power which is God and that we are the products of His creative will. We go on to say that we are more than bodies. We are Soul and Mind, that God can dwell within us and that He can use us to manifest His love and His truth. I suggest now that we read together some chapter in the New Testament to get on closer terms with this subject of the Christian faith. Let's read some words of Jesus. The Salvation Army was founded on His life and teaching and here are three of us seeking to know Him better and serve Him to our heart's satisfaction. Now, what shall we read?"

Len: "The Salvation Army officer here gave me a copy of St. John. This one! Can we read this Gospel? I'll be glad to know more about it."

Frank: "Of course! See how the Gospel begins.

" 'In the beginning was the Word and the Word was with God and the Word was God.—In Him was Life and the Life was the Light of men.'

"Try to get a mental picture of Him, of His looking upon you now with love and understanding and tenderness. Open your heart to Him. Tell Him you need Him urgently in your life, that you want to follow His way, that you seek His forgiveness. Confide all your need to Him and claim that His strength is sufficient for you. Now turn over the pages to chapter fifteen.

" 'I am the Vine, ye are the branches.—Love one another as I have loved you.—I have chosen you and ordained you that ye should go and bring forth more fruit, that your fruit should remain.'

"What do you think of that? You see, Jesus spoke as no man had ever spoken before. He has given us an ideal for living which is unsurpassed. Think seriously over those words of His. The trouble with so many of us is that we tend to obscure His simple teachings in the use of myriad words, vague interpretations and definitions. When you hear Jesus speaking and praying, listen carefully to His expressions. When you do that God becomes very real, doesn't He? His followers saw God in and through Him. How can man have invented God in the light of what Jesus says about Him, what He did in his lifetime? People all down the ages have seen the glory of God in the face and life of Jesus. They have claimed a fellowship with Him that has given them the privilege of calling themselves the children of God. Now look religiously at the Cross of Christ. As He hangs there you can say with earnest conviction, 'He loved me and gave Himself for me.' You'll never find the sure answer to the Cross in the light of cold logic or abstract reason. Religion is not a bargain with God, that is, if you'll say your prayers, pay your dues, He will contract to look after you. No! Face up to Christ quietly and lovingly. Set aside your doubts and hesitancies. Dismiss your fears and suspicions. Let Him release His Power through you, make you a channel of peace and joy and harmony, His agent and partner. I'm afraid I'm speaking too much."

Sid: "No you're not! I was thinking as you were speaking that this place is rightly called—'The Bridge'. It's a bridge between man and God, isn't it?"

Len: "I heard a chap in the open air once say that there was nothing original in what Jesus said, in His teaching and so on. That He was only repeating what others before Him had said. What's the answer to that one?"

Frank: "Long before Jesus there were, of course, outstanding men who said some wise things. Some of their sayings were very like what Jesus proclaimed in His own time. Messages about loving one's neighbour and being merciful and pure and upright. It would be astonishing, wouldn't it, if wise people didn't say something similar to each other in the course of their life history? But don't forget this. It was left to Jesus, not only to live His own teaching to the highest degree of perfection, but also to die to prove it true. He demonstrated His striking uniqueness in this way. There's a Scriptural text which says—'He was obedient unto death.' Jesus was undoubtedly the Son of God in human form, and that in Him and through Him God the Father showed man the way of redemption and salvation. I hope that doesn't sound a bit too complicated or theological. What it comes to is this. Jesus has revealed to us the certainty of God and that no power on earth can separate us from the love of God. That is undiluted truth, not a cunning devised fable. Now we can walk with Christ, live with Him, claim from Him forgiveness of our sins, feel a sense of security unshaken by the storms of life or the terrors of death. Being endowed with free-will, that power of choice rests with us. We can reject Him; we can accept Him. If we reject Him we can go on living a life without direction or purpose, a life of barrenness, vacillation and weakness. If we accept Him I am certain that we are going to experience life filled with happy service and serene confidence. We are going to say—'I know in Whom I have believed.' 'I know Jesus as my Saviour and I will follow Him to the end of the journey.' So what choice are we going to make?"

Several times after that we met together while I was in Wellington city. My new friends attended all my public meetings, Salvation Army services and Youth For Christ rallies. They literally stepped out of their old selves into new physical and spiritual creations. Daily I saw them truly and exultantly discovering Christ as the dynamic power of God to save, heal and bless them in abundance. Both entered into a rich experience of Christian conversion, conversion which washed away from their souls the strong obstructions of ingrained alcoholic habits, which cleansed them from every impulse to drink themselves into degradation and death, and which induced them to share with others the most exhilarating joy they had ever known. They became loving, considerate and grateful. When they shook hands with people, their faces just brimmed with inner glory as if they were proudly announcing their engagement or forthcoming marriage. The Father-God was undoubtedly more to them than a Name. He was their mighty Deliverer, their Shield and their Song.

Sid went back again to his accountancy and attended Salvation Army meetings. His officer said about him—"I like to have him right in front of me when I'm preaching because his radiant face looking up helps me to preach the truly great, uttermost Gospel."

Len went across to Hobart, in Tasmania, and became a successful salesman both for his firm and for his newly-discovered Lord. Recently he sent me his church magazine. I was warmed by reading his recorded Christian testimony and especially his closing paragraphs.

"One afternoon in 'The Bridge', Wellington, after thinking much about what I had heard from a visiting minister and reading my Bible, I knew a change in my life was near. I went to my bedroom, fell on my knees before God and prayed. I told God I was going to stay on my knees until He had truly saved me. As I knelt there God sent Jesus to me. I knew that. He gave me a new life. I said to Him—'All right, Lord! Now I'm yours. You take me and I take You.' I stopped going down to the grave, arranging my own funeral. Now, it's the glad music of the royal march in Christ Jesus. For the rest of my days I am His and He is mine for ever. One day I shall look in His face. I want to go to Him like a victor over many enemies. I want to go to His home to the sound of the trumpet, to the beating of heavenly drums."

Forthright, buoyant, life-enriching stuff. Len, like Sid, had found the Saviour Christ to be a living, redeeming, dynamic Power. He had discovered the powerful Truth which set him free, the only Truth which emancipates men and nations and brings them within the orbit of universal love, healing and peace.

Chapter 7

JESUS SAID: "KEEP MY COMMANDMENTS."

THE liner *Orcades* was four days out from Sydney and was due to reach Manila in another three days. After a heavy series of speaking engagements in Australia and New Zealand, I was glad of the relaxation which the sea voyage offered and spent most of the daylight hours on the top promenade deck reading and occasionally conversing with new friends. Shipping companies in these feverish pleasure-laden days do not, unfortunately, provide "silence rooms" for those of their passengers who desire to keep an armistice of the soul in order to hear the still small voice of God. The constant emphasis is on man's material senses, and the daily entertainment programme caters almost wholly for those who clamour for "something going on" to fill in their many vacant hours and relieve the tedium of their boredom.

On the second morning, going to my favourite spot on the top deck, I observed a woman reclining in a deck-chair nearby watching me closely, her eyes alight with eager curiosity. I nodded to her in greeting and resumed my seat. I was not anxious to appear in any way pressing and thought that if the woman wanted to share with me some secret of her life she would make known her wish. In the afternoon and the following day she was in her usual place, her eyes searching me whenever I looked up, her whole manner suggestive of troubled thought. By this time I was truly intrigued, wondering who she was, why she sat alone, and what were her thoughts. On the fourth morning I found out. My fellow voyager rose from her seat and came across to me.

"Will you excuse me?" she said shyly. "I felt I must speak to you. You are a parson, aren't you? I saw your name in the passenger list and I have one of your books at home. Is it all right for me to talk to you? I mean, I hope I'm not intruding."

"Of course you're not," I answered. "I'll get your chair and bring it here."

Sitting close to me I judged her to be in her middle forties. Her face was very pale and tired. Deep lines of worry furrowed her cheeks and forehead. She was soberly dressed. When I drew up her chair she sank into it with a sigh of utter weariness.

"Well now, what's it all about?" I asked. "You look as if you're carrying a heavy burden. Let me share it with you. Just tell me what you like. Maybe I can help you. Let's see!"

A moment later I was listening to a very familiar story about a husband and wife who had both found marriage to be a hideous nightmare. My companion had foolishly been a partner in a runaway love affair. She knew that her ardent lover had been a prodigious sower of wild oats, but very much swayed by blind passion and innocently believing that she could reform him once they were together, entirely contrary to the good advice of parents and friends, she married him. They set up home together in an upper flat in Sutton, Surrey. From the outset the husband's reformation did not follow the pattern she had planned. Once the first experiences of married bliss were over she was told in very blunt terms that he had no desire to be reformed, that he was quite satisfied with his few mild sins and that she had taken him for better or for worse.

Daily she became more and more shocked by his true character. Soon he came home the worse for drink and the little abode which she had lived for and took affectionate pride in creating, became a storm centre of the most painful and disruptive kind. For a while, after the birth of her first child, the relationship between them improved. The coming of a baby girl into the home induced in the husband a sense of responsibility and self-discipline. He became devoted to his daughter and inspired in the wife a heartening thought that their marriage might yet become the complete harmonious comradeship she had hoped and dreamed it might be. Then, once more, terribly sudden and alarming, the bottom of her world of promise and expectancy dropped right out. Her man arrived home one memorable night, angrily and violently drunk. Everything approaching reason and regard seemed to have snapped within him. He subjected his wife, not only to high bitter words, but also to brutal blows. The oncoming weeks and months confirmed her worst fears that he had fallen victim to a loose band of men and women, that he was unfaithful to her in the most flagrant way and that she was living in a home of snarling domestic tragedy. Taking time to contemplate the inevitable, cruel results, she eventually packed a few things and, with her child, left to live with relatives. It was not an ideal environment, but at least her bed-sitting room did provide for herself and child an atmosphere of peace and love.

A year passed, a year of contentment, a year in which she was able to pay her way by small jobs of typing and baby sitting. Women's ways and thoughts very often run counter to all axioms of cold logic. When her husband began to write to her, pleading for her return to him, saying he was a reformed character and that she would have no reason to complain about his future conduct, she willingly believed him. After a few meetings in which he was fulsome in his promises to make amends for his past, she returned to him. It was soon evident to her that his honeyed words were deceptive subterfuges to get her back. Bitter quarrels again became a common occurrence. Her husband was still a prisoner to liquor and his drunken carousals increased with the oncoming months. Then she found there was to be another baby, a discovery which by no means filled her with rapture. She faced the galling fact that her marriage had to be accepted as a distressing failure, and settled with her husband that they should live separate lives under the same roof. For the sake of the children she would not leave him. She would prepare his meals but keep to her own rooms and remain a wife in name only. The unpleasant pact made, she saw little of him. He continued to drink and gamble heavily and stayed out late at night.

One evening, seated in front of her small television set, Billy Graham came on to the screen. She found herself looking and listening intently to what he was saying.

"Are you really satisfied with your life?" he asked. "Can you truly say you have made a fine success of it? I don't mean success in terms of money and position standards. There is much more in life than mere money-making, than having a safe job. Life is poor stuff unless you know something of the Christian miracle of peace and pardon and power. All of us need God in this world. It may seem easy to bow God out of this life, but there is greater difficulty in getting rid of the devil. When I'm sick and sad and know that I've sinned greatly before God and man, I don't want goods or money. I want the Grace of God that will meet my urgent need, that will give me the strength to be strong again and forgiveness for my many sins. When I know that God loves me and proves it by sending Jesus to be my Saviour and Friend, then I feel that life has glory and purpose in it. There is no other way to right relationships between man and man, between man and woman, than the plain and certain way of Jesus Christ. Jesus loves you, my friend. Why not accept His love tonight and know the blessing of life peace and joy and healing?"

She realised then how much she needed God, the God Who is like Jesus, the God Who is to be found in Jesus. Thinking seriously that she had invited most of her troubles by living life on a low level, by keeping God out of her married partnership, she resolved to turn over a new leaf, to try the Christian way of life. Two nights later, taking the children with her, she went to Harringay Arena, and when the evangelist said that she and everyone else present could experience the exhilarating and emancipating miracle of a Christian new birth, she was one of the first to get up and go forward to the enquiry room and there, unreservedly, she surrendered herself, body and soul, to Jesus Christ.

She knew that a great moral and spiritual change had taken place in her life. She was inwardly happy and sought opportunities to witness for her new-found Lord. When she told her husband about her Christian conversion he laughed derisively and called her a goody-goody simpleton, a pious church baby. On one occasion, seeing her reading the Bible to her two children, he grabbed it, threw it down and stamped on it. That hurt her but she continued to bear her Christian testimony both inside and outside the home.

The narration of my companion's human story took up most of the morning hours. We had to endure many interruptions. Other friends came round with a kindly word.

D

Frequently we were asked to join in games of shuffle-board and deck tennis. More than once we had to seek a quieter spot because thoughtless, noise-loving passengers brought along their transistor radio sets, placed them nearby and tortured our ears with blaring dance music and shrieking rock-and-roll misnamed singers. We arranged to meet again the following morning.

As she came forward to meet me in another secluded spot I had found on the top deck, I was shocked by her changed appearance. Her face was badly puffed up by recent bruises. One eye was blackened. A blood scab surmounted her left eyebrow. I sensed too that she had been crying for some time. Diffidently she held out her hand in greeting and whispered a muffled "Good morning!" Eagerly she took the chair I drew up for her and sat for several moments in pained silence. I thought it wise to remain quiet myself, to let her explain the reason for her facial bruising.

"You're wondering of course how I got this," she said sadly, dabbing a hand quickly to her face. "It's hideous, isn't it? Last night, after I went to my cabin, a spasm of bitterness went through me. 'O God,' I prayed, 'let me die!' That was silly. I'm feeling better now and can face up to any trial that awaits me in the future. I mean, I want to prove the strength of my Christian faith whatever I have to go through."

She paused for a moment then went on:

"You see, this unfortunate experience I went through last night is related to what I was telling you yesterday morning. After my conversion, I wrote to my sister who lives in Bondi, near Sydney, to share the good news with her. She's a fine Christian woman and does a lot of deaconess work there. She invited me to spend a holiday with her. I got a part-time office job, saved a little, flew over, stayed six weeks with her family, then caught this boat back at Sydney. Soon after I came on board I received an unexpected shock. In the gangway on D deck I ran into someone I certainly didn't expect to see. Whom d'you think? My husband. I had told him of course about this holiday, and as he wanted nothing to do with the children —he's often said they're mine, not his—my mother kindly offered to take them. So I felt free to make the trip. I was told by my husband in England, and again last night, that he didn't believe my story. He said I had some secret lover somewhere whom I had come to see. So he actually left his job, came over in some other ship and booked this one at home for the return passage, knowing I would be on it. What do you think of that? He didn't trust me and has spent a lot of his money on this foolhardy quest. Last night, when I was in the laundry ironing out a few clothes, he came in. Unfortunately, I was alone. He had been drinking and wanted a row. He called me a religious humbug and a lot of other stupid things, used some horrible swear-words and suddenly started to hit me. I was helpless. Fortunately, some other woman turned up and he went off snarling and cursing to himself."

She ended abruptly, jerked her head back and gave me a strained look. Then, to my embarrassment, she hung her head down and burst into loud sobbing. Her whole body was convulsed, and blinding tears poured from her eyes. The protracted strain of dealing with a difficult, antagonistic husband had finally broken her. For a good five minutes her intense crying continued. Then, gradually, she regained her normal composure. Slowly she lifted her head and looked at me with tear-dimmed eyes.

"I'm sorry about this," she said hesitantly. "It's silly of me. Anyhow, I feel better now. Only I don't like this face of mine."

"Don't worry, my dear," I replied. "Those bruises will soon disappear. Like St. Paul, you're carrying the marks of your Christian conflict about with you. You know the saying—'to do and to endure.' The Christian life is a strenuous battle, isn't it? You, like the rest of us, have your testing times, and you're seeking to show the reality of your Christian faith not by lips alone but in life. But we have a duty to you too, that is, to protect you from your unreasonable, pugilistic husband. Your face was not given you to be his punching bag. When you go to your cabin, wait, if you can, for someone going your way, so that you're not alone. Maybe, one day on the ship, I can run into him and have a chat. Who knows! Some good may yet come out of this queer spying venture of his."

Little did I realise then that a simple word of this kind, so loaded with hope, would soon reap a fruitful harvest.

I told my tearful companion, whose Christian name I discovered was Irene, that I had been asked by several friends on board to conduct a spiritual retreat on two mornings a week for an hour, and had permission to hold it in the children's nursery. I invited her to come. Some twenty or so people turned up for our first meeting. I announced then that I would speak on God is Love and at successive gatherings on God is Light, God is Peace, God is Power, God is Mercy, God is Life, and so on.

"Beloved, let us love one another, for love is of God." We considered the supreme truth in life that Jesus expressly came to tell people that God's name and nature was Love. His love was under them, over them, around them, inside of them. His love redeems, transforms, uplifts. It brings out the best in the human heart, creates faith, inspires hope, engenders service. No home or life can fail where God's love abides. If a man gains the whole world and is lacking in love, his life is but a mockery. God is anxious to make our hearts His endearing home. With Him as our daily Lover, Guide and Companion, we can experience a life of uplifting service, abiding peace and heart satisfaction. We can look into His face and smile the smile of complete trust and abandon.

Some three evenings later, strolling round the promenade deck, I caught the sounds of raucous shouting, of high-pitched, angry voices. Approaching an alcove wherein was a refreshment bar, I saw a tall, thick-shouldered, red-faced man, obviously tipsy, standing among a group of men and women passengers, holding a beer glass in his hand. He was using bad language and attempting to paw one of the women. While others pushed and bawled at him, he lifted his glass and drunkenly called out: "This is my medicine," drank some of it and threw the rest of it in the face of the lady nearest to him. Instantly, pandemonium broke out. He was felled by the fist of one of the men; the glass flew from his hand and was broken into tiny pieces, and as he sprawled on the deck others of the company pummelled and kicked him. Amidst the noisy clamour and confusion the bar attendants moved in and restored order. In the morning, Irene informed me she had heard that her husband had been caught up in a scuffle, was badly beaten up, and by doctor's orders was confined to his bed. She would like to see him but was a little afraid to do so in case he tried again to treat her with violence. Here was my God-given opportunity to do a little good for both of them.

"I'll go and see him," I said earnestly. "I expect the ship's purser will be glad to use me as a chaplain, to visit the sick and infirm. What's his cabin number? Meet me up here tonight after dinner and I'll let you know how I got on."

My invalid was in a two-berth cabin down on E deck.

I wore my clerical collar so that he should know I was on
a pastoral visit. Receiving a brusque "Come in" in response
to my knock, my entrance was greeted with a low whistle
and an exclamation—"Cor blimey!" I smiled and shook
hands with him. He was sitting up in bed reading an old
newspaper. His face was pulpy with several bloody gashes.
The physical ill-treatment he had bestowed on his wife
had been returned to him by others a hundredfold.

"Why this unexpected honour?" he asked sharply. "A
sky pilot, eh, to see a poor old broken boozer like me! Am
I that important?"

I drew up the cabin chair and sat facing him.

"I'm Padre Jennings," I said cheerfully. "I heard that
one of my ship's passenger flock had been wounded on
the field of battle, so I felt it my duty to come and see
him. Well, how are you?"

At once, his attitude of animosity changed to one of
friendliness. He evidently did appreciate my visit and was
anxious to show me courtesy and good will.

"You know, padre," he said, putting his newspaper aside
and attempting a grin, "I haven't spoken to one of your
cloth for years, not since I got married and that wasn't
for long. It's good of you to come and see me. I've been
thinking a lot since the old doc. told me I had to stay in
bed. No sleep last night. Too much pain all over me. What
a fool! And all my own fault. What d'you think of that?
You know how I got this, don't you? Too much bottling
and tippling. That's me! Fancy, asking for all this trouble
simply because I can't control myself. Man to man I'm
telling you that. Yes, a blankety fool—to myself, my wife
and everybody else. If I had more sense I wouldn't be
here. I mean, on this ship. I'm crazy, I tell you. I begin
drinking and I've got plenty of money to keep on at it.
I keep on until I'm properly fuddled. Then I start knock-

ing people about. I don't blame 'em for resisting and setting on to me. That's what happened here. They beat me up because I asked for it. Result—a badly bruised face and body, a thorough hiding, a good fee for the doctor, a nuisance to other passengers and, with it all, estrangement from my wife and family. A lovely life, isn't it?"

I certainly never expected our conversation to follow this line. I anticipated meeting a very difficult, cantankerous man. Yet here was one who seemed eager to be chummy and self-informative, who wasn't backward in admitting his reckless, stupid follies. It was abundantly evident that his bar companions had not only badly pummelled his face; they had, as well, driven some solid common sense into his mind. I felt that I could trade on his forthright manly confessions to bring him face to face with life's highest realities. Meanwhile I deemed it wise to encourage him to keep on talking, to convince him that I was certainly interested in his general well-being. "Where have you been on this voyage?" I asked. "Are you stepping off at Hong Kong or Kobe or Vancouver or going right through to Tilbury? You're not Australian, are you?"

"Me, Australian? Heavens no! Although I wouldn't mind being one. Good chaps the cobbers. Where have I been on this trip? Nowhere! I boarded her at Sydney. Stayed a few days there. Came over on a Dutch boat. I thought a sea trip might be good for my health. Look at me! Doesn't seem to have done me much good, does it? Ought to have done, you know! I spent a heck of a lot of money on it. I don't mind that. I'm not short in the money line. But what I do mind and ought to mind is that I'm such a fat-headed chump. I'm my own enemy, always have been. I've a screw loose, that's my trouble."

He laughed out loud and smacked the newspaper with his hand.

"But you needn't always have a screw loose," I answered. "You know I'm a padre. Why? Because I believe in a Power which can put right what is wrong in our lives, both yours and mine. Why shouldn't I be like you? You admit to being a tippler; you can't control yourself; you get into fights. What's to stop me following your example? Because I use the sanity God has given me, because I recognised long ago that Christianity tightens a man's moral, physical and spiritual screws, counters his innate selfishness and folly with strong doses of reason, goodness and power. That's sane, practical, down-to-earth Christianity. That's why Jesus came to this earth, why you have churches, why people become Christians. Why don't you become a Christian? You will never regret it, you know. By the way, what's your Christian name?"

"Call me Jack! Me a Christian? Don't make me laugh, padre. That's not in my line. Me singing hymns all day long on Sunday, going to church, perhaps taking up the collection! Oh no! I like my drink and a good swear and gamble sometimes. I can't see myself in a white shirt yet. I'm a man, not an angel."

He made a guffawing noise and, as far as his swollen face allowed, tried to grin at me. I liked his utter frankness, his friendly disposition, even his simple mistaken idea of the Christian faith. It was plainly evident that he had not given much thought to it.

"Jack, let all my words be kindly. I'm here to help you. You know that, don't you? I don't want to force my Christian faith on to you. You do realise that, I'm sure."

"Of course I do. I'm enjoying this talk. Say what you like. I don't suppose a chat about religion will do me any harm."

"It will do both of us a lot of good. Religion, that is the Christian religion, is mankind's greatest benefactor.

Have you ever thought of that, Jack? It stands for all the best you know of in life. Think of the evils that are turning this world into a bear garden, that are causing men to behave as human animals, to be immoral, to cheat, to lie, to give themselves sexual licence, to behave as foul louts and bullies. What's the answer to that? What's the answer to that low-down rotter who coshed the bank messenger the other day, robbed him of a lot of money and left him bleeding and unconscious on the pavement? Was that rotter a Christian? Far from it! Supposing he had been one, would he have attacked the bank fellow and before doing so prayed a prayer to God for success in his wicked mission? Would he? Don't you see, Jack, if lots more people were definitely Christian, true followers of Jesus Christ, this world would be a much better, happier place to live in. There would be a lot less misery and crime and hatred and crying everywhere!"

He riveted his eyes on me all the time I was speaking and rutted his brows as if thinking deeply over what I was saying. I waited a second for him to speak but instead he nodded to me to continue.

"All right! God is trying to bring righteousness and peace into this world. He's a Father and a Lover to us, Jack. Jesus came to tell us that. If only we would love and serve God, then the old devil wouldn't stand much chance to work his evil will, would he? But man is free and God respects His freedom. Man can commit evil if he wants to and does, in spite of God. When we open our lives to Christ, my friend, we can't do much ill. The heart of Christianity isn't singing many hymns, just going to church, although we ought to do that, or even taking up the collection as you say. It's the acceptance of a very beautiful and universal truth, that we live and move and have our being in God, that He loves us and that we can love and serve Him in return. That's real life, Jack, the highest ideal and purpose in life, good for the home, for happiness, for laughter, for love. God didn't mean you to have a bruised body and a smashed face, to spend some lonely hours here in bed. Oh no! What's to stop you turning over a new leaf and living your life under His guiding control? What about it?"

He gave me a searching look, swallowed a bit, hesitated for a moment as if seeking to find words to express his thoughts.

"You say a mouthful, don't you, padre?" he said, throwing a hand in my direction. "But I admit you've got something. I've never thought of it in that light. I mean this Christian set-up. Perhaps if I had had it explained to me like that a few years ago I wouldn't have gone off the rails as I have. By George, you've given me plenty to think about, haven't you? Well, I can take it."

"It's never too late to mend a sinful life, Jack. Now is the accepted time to allow Jesus Christ to be your Saviour and Friend for the rest of your days. Well now, that's enough to go on with. It's tea-time. I'll ask the steward to bring you something. Would you like me to come and see you tomorrow afternoon?"

"Rather! We're getting on like a house on fire, aren't we? I shall be singing a solo at your service next Sunday the way we're going. What shall I sing? 'Another Little Drink Won't Do Us Any Harm!'"

He burst out in an explosion of laughter which was both captivating and contagious. I found myself laughing heartily with him.

Irene was greatly surprised and overjoyed when I told her the result of my visit and that I was expected to see him again. I thought it wise for her to wait another day or so before calling to see her husband in the hope that I could tactfully bring her into our conversation if he did not refer to her. I had the impression that he was not anxious for her to meet him in his sad, gory condition.

The next afternoon I was back again in his cabin and this time I took with me two of my books—*Men of the Lanes,* the account of my specialised ministry among tramps, gypsies, showmen and circus folk, and *Calvary Covers it All,* stories of men I had contacted in my own missions who had found their lives transformed by the miraculous saving power of Jesus Christ. I told him something of my world-wide travels, of my experiences with gentlemen of the road. He was intensely interested and asked me numerous questions about my Christian and sociological work. Gradually I switched him over to the claims of Christ on his life and then our conversation continued on the same Christian lines as the day before.

The *Orcades* called at Hong Kong and I spent the two days of our stay there mostly fulfilling speaking engagements. As soon as the ship resailed, I lost no time in going to Jack's cabin. I found my friend looking much better, the swellings and bruises on his face having mostly disappeared. He expressed his pleasure in seeing me again and referred to many incidents he had read in my books.

"Say, you've had quite a life of it, haven't you?" he said brightly. "And some of your experiences! Golly, how unusual and fascinating! I've read these books of yours with great interest. Thanks for passing them on to me. I found them jolly good company lying back here. You know, you've given me quite a different idea of religion. I don't mind telling you I used to think it was all tripe, all right for women and kids but too soppy for men. I've got another idea of it now. It keeps a man straight, doesn't it? Reading about those chaps who had a change over after they became religious made me look into my own life. I don't mind admitting, padre, that last night, thinking of those fellows you've written about, I actually said to myself—'Jack, old man, if you became religious yourself it would do you a basinful of good.' I'm seeing things differently. I thought about those blokes giving up their boozing and rottenness when they became Christians. I liked it. I liked it because they started to alter things, didn't they? You know what I mean, they began to alter things they'd done wrong. And then it was better for everybody. Well, I may not have got it right but I feel this, if religion or Jesus Christ can make a new man of them, I'll let Him have a go at me. Straight I will."

His face lit up with renewed hope and confidence. Before I could say anything he went on speaking:

"I'll tell you something else. I've sunk as low as any human being can do. I've degraded myself. I've done great wrong to my parents, my family, my wife. D'you know, padre, my wife is on board this ship, that I came on it to spy on her, that I actually hit her the other day. Of course I was drunk when I did it. That's what booze does to a man. It hurts me when I think about it. And she's a fine Christian woman, too. I tell you, if I was like her I would be proud of my life. But I'm not. I'm sorry now I haven't been much of a husband to her. But as you say, it's not too late to mend and I would honestly like to make it up to her. I would really. Now I understand this Christian business better, how you've put it and what I've read in these books, somehow I feel I'd like some more instruction about it. You tell me what I have to do to be a Christian. I'm game."

For another hour I talked to him about the heart of the Christian message, how that Christianity is the coming of Jesus into the heart of man, how He comes to indwell in our lives, to reach down into the haunts of secret evil, to release us from the strong clutches of sin, to forgive us our sins, to work an inner cleansing, a change of heart, a transformation of character. He gives us the glorious liberty of the sons of God. He comes to rescue drunkards, gamblers, drug fiends, high-born, low-born, everybody who comes to Him. Nobody is outside His loving care. He lived and died to prove it true.

"Jack, Jesus Christ is the very centre of your being, sufficient for your every need. He is waiting now to fulfil His redemptive work in you. He is in your longing heart, your aching body, your awakening soul, waiting for your call to Him. His hands stretch out to grasp yours; His eyes smile into your eyes. Why not surrender yourself wholly to Him now? Listen to His voice saying 'Come Unto Me!' He is the Resurrection and the Life within you. Open your heart and soul to Him. Just say—'Come into my life, Lord Jesus and make it your abiding home'."

We prayed together, then still on our knees, I asked him again to accept Jesus, the sinner's dearest Friend, as his Lord and Saviour. I waited for a full minute then he spoke the glad words that I was longing to hear.

"Dear Jesus Christ, if you can save a rotter like me, I'm yours from today."

When he stood up to confront me his face was suffused with happiness.

"Something's just happened to me," he said gaily. "I feel reborn."

"So you are. Reborn of God's spirit."

He asked me to tell his wife the glad tidings and to bring her along for a happy reunion the following afternoon. Irene was amazed and dumbfounded when I shared with her the momentous news of her hubby's conversion, and filled with joyous overflowing at the early prospect of meeting him.

She looked very smart and winsome when I met her the next day. There was little trace of her former facial injuries. Jack's cabin door was slightly open when I knocked on it. In an instant it was pulled wide open and Jack, now fully and trimly dressed, bounded forward, shouted "Irene" and swept her into his embrace. He held her very close to him and kissed her with the passion of a man who has newly learned the sacred meaning of love. With arms closely interlocked they stood together for some time, large tears running freely down their cheeks. I turned my head away, inwardly moved. That plain ship's cabin had been suddenly transformed into an annexe of heaven and I had been allowed to step into it. A voice caused me to turn and face them again.

"This is the Lord's doing and it's wonderful," said Irene. "Thank God! Thank God!"

Her face lit up with a sunny tenderness.

"Thanks, Irene," murmured Jack, looking lovingly at her. "Thanks for helping me to see my way to God. I know now. I know that I can't live without Him and get away with it. I've been such a fool, such a fool."

"Both of us have been fools but now, no more. God has forgiven us and now we have to make a fresh start together. I love you and I want you."

"I want you," he replied with vigour. "Don't I just! I want to prove myself a real man to you."

"That's it! God's good man. Let's both dedicate ourselves to Christ and then nothing can come between us."

After a moment's silence she turned swiftly to me.

"Padre, I've got an idea. Is it possible for us to have a kind of wedding service again? I mean, although we're married, could we say those marriage sentences once more now that we understand the real meaning of marriage. I think I'd like that. What do you say, Jack?"

"I'm all for it. Another marriage service? Yes! I didn't understand what it really meant before but I do now. That's a brainy idea. What a fine start for our reunion and for our new home! Yes, let's do that! I've heard of married couples renewing their vows. Let us do it, Irene!"

I gave the matter some consideration and decided that a simple service of re-consecration, using the phrases which form the heart of the marriage service, would be a very inspiring and memorable happening in their future Christian life together. By mutual arrangement, I gathered a few friends and we met in Jack's cabin the following afternoon. Some sat on the twin beds and others on the floor. Jack and Irene stood in front of me. We began with a brief prayer.

"We thank Thee, Our Father, for the sacred institution of marriage. Be pleased to bless these two dear children of Thine who have come here to reconsecrate themselves in their married partnership. May this glad ceremony be the outward and visible sign of an inward and spiritual union, a union of hearts and lives in true godly affection and service. We commit them to Thy loving care and protection throughout their earthly days. In the Name of Jesus we ask it. Amen."

Then they held hands and I asked Jack to repeat after me.

"I call upon these friends present to witness that I, Jack B—— your husband, solemnly and affectionately renew my married vows to you Irene, my dear wife, from this day forward, for better for worse, for richer for poorer, in sickness and in health, to love and to cherish, till death us do part, according to God's holy ordinance, and here now, I pledge to you my dedicated love and companionship all the years God gives us together."

Irene then repeated the same words, substituting wife for husband at the beginning of her vows. Then we all said the Lord's Prayer together and I spoke to them about the Christ Who came to fashion us into new moral, physical and spiritual creations, human, sanctified messengers of victory and joy. When we build our married life, our home life, on the foundation of His love and guidance, then truly, nothing harmful can come between us. "Except the Lord build the house they labour in vain who build it."

Softly we sang "Blessed Assurance, Jesus Is Mine," then I closed with the Benediction. Irene turned happily to me. Her eyes were filled with sparkling light. I knew that a wondrous peace filled her heart, that she felt strong with a new power and experienced the peace beyond understanding. She smiled.

"I am very happy," she said.

Then Jack gripped my hand in a firm grasp.

"Thanks, padre! Who'd have thought it? It staggers me. When I get back home, you know what? I'm going to join Irene's church. We'll serve God together until the end. Trust me."

I said 'Goodbye' to them at Long Beach, California, where I disembarked in order to fulfil some American engagements. They sailed on for home. Letters come to me from them. New life and purpose have flooded them from high heaven and with them mutual happiness in Christ has firmly come.

Chapter 8

JESUS SAID: "I AM THE WAY."

MOIST darkness settled over the dockside area of San Francisco. There was no moon and a low ceiling of heavy, rain-filled clouds raced swiftly across the sky. My progress back to the mission hostel, where I was a welcome guest after speaking at a Salvation Army rally, was hindered by the large number of broken men who staggered out of dingy saloons and flop-houses and others who shuffled along the pavement, endeavouring to sell to passers-by soiled items of clothing, razor blades or cheap watches, for the price of a bottle of cheap whisky or potent methylated spirits. My clerical collar was a powerful magnet for these shambling, reeling down-and-outs. Constantly I was asked to purchase a stained shirt, a greasy sweater, a pair of well-used shoes as well as pleaded with for a nickel, a dime or even a couple of cents. To escape these whining cadgers I crossed the road to a restaurant thinking that a light supper would be welcome. Studying the menu pinned on a board inside the window I was suddenly conscious of someone standing just behind me. An obnoxious smell of stale, alcoholic breath floated over my left shoulder and into my nose.

"Excuse me, sir," came a pleading voice. "Can you help me in some small way? I'm sorry to ask you but I'm really hungry. I haven't eaten today."

I turned quickly and looked into the bloated, furrowed

face of a poorly dressed man. That face with its bleared eyes, its prominent creased cheeks, was loaded with the sorrows of many bitter years. Of medium height, he wore clothes that were threadbare and seedy. Although the wind was piercingly cold and the air damp, he was hatless and his brown shoes were cracked enough to reveal his bare feet.

"I'm sorry to ask you, sir," he mumbled quickly as I confronted him, "but I saw you crossing the road and I felt I had to speak to you. I heard you the other night at the mission and then last night at the Salvation Army Citadel. I know I shouldn't beg, especially from people like you, but I'm almost at my wit's end. But don't mind, sir, saying no."

He spoke in a cultured, educated voice that set me wondering who he was and what he was doing in that frowsy area where habitually a legion of besotted derelicts foregather. A plate of hamburgers and several cups of coffee put him in the mood for friendly conversation. The meal over, he relaxed contentedly and in response to my questioning, began an intensely human story shot through with dogging tragedy, galling defeat and insane folly, a story that he continued to develop in the privacy of my city room whenever I could find time to see him. Encircled by friendship, sympathy and understanding, he laid bare the festering, hurting wounds of his heart, and then, appealingly, asked for counsel and guidance. I am overjoyed to record that his enthralling life narrative had a very happy ending and I want to share this joy with my readers. Let Doctor Cliff tell his verbatim story as he told it to me during his several visits to my mission quarters.

"I was born in Albany, New York State, of well-to-do people. My father was a vice-president of a well-known insurance company and a leading official in the Baptist Church. Constantly we had ministers and missionaries in our house and my good mother entertained them royally. Some of my happiest boyhood years were spent in the church. I sang in the Sunday school choir, joined the Christian Endeavour, and on more than one occasion gave a brief address to the Young People's Bible Class.

"My parents gave me the very best in their power. From a preparatory school I went on to High School where I graduated with honours in a number of subjects. At the age of seventeen, I chose medicine as my life vocation and was trained in New York, going the rounds of the hospitals, especially the City and Belle Vue. In the latter hospital we had a ward for hardened alcoholics and I saw at first-hand the terrific harm that alcohol can do to a man. Surrounded by doctors and by fellow students, mostly older than myself, I felt very happy and self-confident. The world of success, I reckoned, lay at my feet and I was terribly anxious to get out into it and prove myself an indispensable member of society.

"One evening, I joined a party of hospital physicians, students and nurses in a supper dance. Drinks were plentiful, and against my inclination I was persuaded to accept a glass of whisky. I didn't want to be unsociable, so cheerfully and hurriedly I drank the stuff. It was like drinking liquid fire. It scorched my throat and seared the lining of my stomach. I vowed there and then that I would never touch the accursed spirit again. Yet within a week, at another hospital party, there I was quaffing more of it, simply because I wanted to be regarded as a good sport by the others.

"Somehow I managed to pass my medical exams but before doing so, I had to ask my father to pay a few debts I had incurred because I felt compelled to entertain many others in the hospital who had entertained me. This adjunct to good comradeship I considered, called for the abundant use of liquor. You see, by this time my drinking was no longer an occasional habit or a novelty, but a daily occupation. I got to the point where I felt I must take a drink because I needed it. I had to confess to my parents that I was 'on the bottle'. They were very distressed and pleaded with me to quit it. I promised faithfully I would, but with my debts paid and my colleagues clapping me on the back because they regarded me as a fine fellow, I continued drinking.

"I became an assistant to a doctor in Boston. More money to spend and long, tedious hours of work, work which drove my body and mind to the limits of their endurance, caused me to rely more and more on alcohol to keep me going. It took a firm grip on my life and gradually became my master. The Sunday school boy, the church-going lover, actually became alcohol's abject slave. It was not just mid-morning or late night that I wanted it. I desired it many times during the day and recklessly I satisfied my desire. In consequence, my work suffered as well as my health. I was often late for appointments and in my muddled state I frequently gave a wrong diagnosis. There were many complaints about me and after frequent warnings what I sometimes feared actually happened. One always-to-be-remembered morning, after a night's drunken spree, I turned up late at the surgery. My partner was alone. He had attended to all the patients. Coldly he glared at me.

"'I've been waiting for you, old boy,' he said explosively. 'Here is your cheque for the last week. I no longer need you. You have compelled this action. You refused to heed my previous warnings. So, for the good of the profession, I have to dispense with your services.'

"I was out. I slunk back to my digs and considered my position. My drink-clouded mind gradually cleared. I had to face an accusing conscience. Inevitable trouble I had surely asked for. It had certainly come. I had known happiness and success. Foolishly I had exchanged them for abasement and defeat. What a fool I was, a great booze-blinded fool! My ambition and resolve had been drowned in a tidal wave of alcohol. I sat for some time cursing myself for my unforgivable idiocy. Then I made a firm resolution. I would beat this drink devil even if it cost me my life. I wouldn't be mastered by the bottle. Somebody else, yes, but not me. I pulled myself together and went home. I told my parents that I had been unwell, that I was now a teetotaller and that I was looking for a medical partnership with a good Christian man. They were delighted with my sincere intention to turn over a new leaf. Our relationship was radiantly happy. Twice a Sunday for a month I was in church, and life with my dear ones was everything that it should be, good and noble and pure and true.

"I managed to get a partnership with a doctor in Providence, Rhode Island. He was a fine buddy and helped me a lot. But do you know that after I was so confident I had beaten the drink demon, my very cocksureness led to my downfall. Out one evening with some friends I was silly enough to accept a small tot of whisky, saying to myself that it had medicinal value, and that I was now strong enough to resist all further offers of liquor. Before the night was over I was helplessly drunk and my companions had to take me to my quarters in a cab. Gradually, the old craving for alcohol returned, and every open saloon bar was a pressing invitation to go in and have a quick one. My partner, open-eyed to my drunken habits, was very patient and talked to me seriously for my own good. I made many promises and resolutions and, of course, meant to keep them. But soon I realised that I was a mere pawn in the hands of merciless alcoholic forces which had got me in their vicious clutches. I'm quite sure now that had I stayed on in that city my long-suffering partner would have been forced to sack me as the first one did. Fortunately for me this didn't happen, for the Second World War gave me an opportunity to resign and join the American Army as a doctor. I served in the Far East campaigns and finished up in Japan. I need hardly tell you that I found plenty of facilities for indulging my drink cravings while in the army. My booze bills in the officers' mess were always stiff, and often I was reprimanded by my medical superiors for appearing on duty in an inebriated condition.

"The war over, I decided to buy a medical practice, try to pull myself together and settle down. I'm sorry to tell you that my moral condition wasn't all that it ought to have been. Drink, as you may know, is closely allied to sex, and a drunken man has little will power to resist temptation to immorality. But I thought with a home and practice of my own I could sober up, behave myself and become a good husband and citizen.

"Then I made a bad blunder. I married disastrously. After I had acquired a small practice in Seattle, Washington, and had cut down my liquor consumption a good deal, I looked round for a suitable marriage partner. I got to know a woman who was in business in the city. She was fairly attractive, had a little money and appeared to possess a quiet and co-operative disposition. How ghastly wrong I was! Our acquaintanceship was far too short and during it, I paid some of her debts and too readily believed her tales about others who supposedly had been unkind and cruel to her.

"In making her my wife I did the worst thing I could possibly have done. It was a crime against common sense.

I committed social, intellectual and spiritual suicide. I soon discovered that she had a fiendish temper, was densely ignorant regarding elementary knowledgeable subjects, was utterly selfish and could show her claws when thwarted. There was absolutely nothing in tune between us. It was impossible to talk to her about art or music or religion or books. She had no mind for these themes and wasn't one bit interested. Her main interest was money she could get from me. She would laugh at what she called my "cranky idealism" and insult me both in public and private. Her behaviour and language were pretty foul and I had to do something about it. You can't build a home life on the basis of constant mistrust and quarrelling, can you? My nerves were shot to hell. Not surprising, I took increasingly to drink in order to drown my disgust and sorrow. It couldn't go on. The situation might have led to dire tragedy. I had to get rid of her, so I sold my practice and came to this state so as to make a fresh start. Do you know that fifty per cent of the Skid Row population are here because of mis-fit marriages? Why do we make these awful mistakes? Why are so many men so easily deceived by women?"

He stopped abruptly in his sad narrative because I could see he was choking with emotion. His mouth twisted with bitterness. His eyes were blurred with tears. From his pocket he took out a dirty handkerchief and wiped them, then blew his nose loudly. He looked the picture of pathetic, faded misery. I waited a few moments for him to continue but he glared earnestly at me and requested an answer to his challenging questions.

"I believe in the sacred character of the marriage bond," I said, "but I recognise only too well that many marriages —so called—should never have been allowed to take place. The people entering into them, by their very low animal nature and design, are not fit to enter into matrimony. Numerous married couples make a mockery of holy wedlock. Those who talk about the sacrament of marriage ought to remember the myriads who don't regard it as such. Marriage is a great risk for either. One of them can be outrageously deceived. A marriage without love, loyalty, honour and purity can be a hell on earth and ought not to be perpetuated. It is not Christianity to condemn the innocent to life-long misery, to deny them a second chance of happiness when a previous marriage has ended in disaster. For far too many men and women, marriage is nothing more or less than legalised lust. It is not necessary that a man and his wife should have all their tastes and interests in common but it is imperative that there should be a dominant, co-ordinating factor at work in their lives. When that factor is a spiritual one I should say the marriage can hardly go wrong. It is this exclusion of the spiritual from the world of the physical that causes most of the domestic unhappiness that surrounds us. How many couples entering into matrimony consider the question of spiritual fitness for it? Very few, I'm positive. The strains of the Wedding March do not hallow a church marriage which, lacking the necessary essentials of Christian love, fidelity and respect, is nothing more than a prelude to an unworthy act approaching wickedness."

He nodded vigorously in agreement as I spoke but I was anxious to hear the rest of his sorrowful story so motioned for him to proceed.

"Thank you for those truthful words," he said, as he leaned forward watching me closely. "Naturally, I had to start all over again when I came here. In California you have to go to a medical school for a period in order to get a State licence to practise. So, after brushing up my medical knowledge, I went into another partnership, this time in Los Angeles. For a time all went well. I was still drinking but able to carry out all my duties. Then came the day when I was stupid enough to accept a big fee for an illegal operation. The girl died and I was charged with malpractice. Well, that was the end of my career as a doctor. I was completely barred from practice and once more, was out on the street. What to do I didn't know. I had saved a little money but with big living expenses, that didn't last long. I had to turn my hand to any job I could get. Do you know that with all my first-class education and medical degrees I've known many a day like the one when I accosted you in the street, when I've had to beg because I was very hungry and I hadn't a nickel to my name. The jobs I've done since I was turfed out of my medical world! I've been a gasoline attendant, a door-to-door salesman for refrigerators and other kitchen ware, the manager of a bowling alley, an office employee in a motor factory, a book seller, a bottle washer in several saloons, a road labourer, a brass polisher and very many more. What haven't I done to keep a few clothes on my back and to get a few dollars to satisfy my craving for alcohol? I have been astonished at the depths to which I could sink in order to get enough for a bottle of booze.

"Padre, listen! Very often I've been so raving mad for booze that I've gone to a reliever shop and sold my good clothes for filthy ragged ones! They made me look like a devil-born pauper. Then I've managed to fix a few odd jobs, sobered up a bit and bought myself a decent suit and a few underclothes. After a few weeks the old Sneaky Pete or Pink Lady demon would possess me and, astounding it may seem, back I went to the reliever's and traded my good clothes for some scallywag ones and a little money. Yes, and I've seen the day when I've got so low in self-respect and decency that I've actually gone down these Skid Row streets panhandling, my good shirt in one hand and my nice coat in the other, actually trying to get a few nickels for them. What for? You don't have to guess twice. I've looked at other panhandlers, at dopes staggering out of saloons and others asleep in doorways, and I've said to myself—'Cliff, old man, you're one of them. You've willingly joined the legion of the damned. You're broken. You're a hell-bound no-good.'"

After one of his visits to me he settled back in his chair, eagerly accepted the light meal I gave him, then, in response to my appeal to him to continue to unburden himself completely of his past, to tell me anything he liked so that I could help him, he gave me a look heavy with sadness, then relaxed into silence. Because of the impressive quietness in my room the small clock on the mantelshelf seemed to tick very loud. Life suddenly seemed to have gone grey. When my companion spoke, his voice was very low and uncertain. He seemed to be in the grip of strong emotion.

"I'm glad to come here," he said with evident feeling. "I've nowhere else to go. Keeps me out of the saloons—that is, when I've got a dime or two to spend in them. But I'm sorry I've bored you with my wretched story. Last night in my lousy bed in the flophouse I could see that I'm finished. I know something about abortion. Well, my thirst for drink has brought abortion to my career. I know that I'm done for. I'm just a pawn at the mercy of vicious forces I can't contend with. I'll tell you something. I have tried to beat this terrible disease in my life. It is a disease. I've been into five different alcoholic hospitals. In the last one they took the trouble to give me a thorough examination. The senior surgeon told me this: 'You got alcoholic cirrhosis of the liver, old man. Your abdomen is badly swollen. You may as well know the plain truth. Go on drinking as you do now and you'll be dead within a year. Maybe less. You're surely killing yourself.' That's what he said to me and as an ex-medical man, I know he's right. Well, I feel there's nothing now for me to live for. I've come to life's terminus, the miserable end of what promised to be a brilliant life. All I want now is to go on drinking, just sleeping and drinking until—they find me dead. I've already buried all my ambition and hope. So let me go to the grave dishonoured and disgraced. That's my very near home. I'm on my way to bury the dead—myself."

He flopped back in his chair. His shoulders were sadly bent, his face torn and agitated with inner distress. His whole body visibly trembled. He buried his face in his hands and began to cry quietly. After a minute or two his sobs ended. With his soiled handkerchief he wiped his eyes then looked across at me, his face eloquent with suffering appeal.

"I know I'm down," he blurted, "but am I right out? Am I? Is there no hope for me? That fellow in the Bible who lived among the swine! Didn't he manage to get away from his stinking piggery? He did, didn't he? Can't I do it? Tell me I can! Oh God, please!"

Once more he convulsed into agonised crying but this time his sobs were loud and painful. He was a completely broken man. He was being tortured by his many accusing sins. It was time for me to take over. I went across to him and put my arm around his shoulder.

"Yes, Cliff! That prodigal in the Bible did get out of his piggery. He left his old swinish life, went home and became a new man. So can you. You belong to God. In His love and care you can certainly make a fresh start."

For about half an hour I talked to him quietly about the dynamic power of the Christian faith, how it was related to the warm heart of humanity with its multiplicity of cares, sorrows, temptations, failures, hopes and aspirations. It was centred in the living, transforming Person of Jesus Christ. He came to save us from our sin. Sin was the biggest enemy of man. Jesus deals with the root cause of all unhappiness. We can all go to Him for a new start, especially the most hopeless and despairing. He gives new strength to the weak will, new sight to the blind, new understanding of life's highest mission.

I asked my ex-doctor friend to turn over his drinking problem, and all his other problems, entirely to Christ. He would eagerly take them over and release him from the burden of sin that had become too heavy for him to bear. Tens of thousands of other alcoholics just like him had experienced a marvellous change in their lives the very minute they decided to stop trying to stay sober by their own efforts and let Jesus take over the management. I pleaded with him to give it a try.

He remained very still while I talked, seemingly very receptive to what I was saying. Occasionally, as I spoke, a soft moan escaped from his lips. When he did reply, which appeared to cost him a great effort, he was full of contrition that he had not heeded earnest advice given to him by well-meaning friends, turned his eyes away from the light of decency and sanity and blinded himself of true moral and spiritual values. Had he listened to the voice of wisdom, kept a little place in his life for God, what many bitter and painful years of defeat, degradation and suffering he would have been spared.

That night I secured him a bed in a small private hotel. He was away from the filth and contamination of a corrupting flophouse. The next morning mission friends took charge of him, fed and re-clothed him. In the evening I preached in the Salvation Army Citadel. As I looked from the platform on that dismal human sea of sin-scarred,

unwashed faces, men huddled in their seats, scrubby chins
sunk on their chests, eyes roaming with dull hopelessness
on nothing, I spied my friend Cliff sitting with a group of
better-dressed men, recent converts, expectant and alive.
With commendable earnestness and enthusiasm we sang
our opening hymn.

> *God will take care of you, be not afraid,*
> *He is your safeguard thro' sunshine and shade.*
> *Tenderly watching and keeping his own,*
> *He will not leave you to wander alone.*

A short prayer, Bible reading on the Prodigal Son, a few
stirring, lilting choruses, then the address. I found myself
saying:

"The greatest, positive truth for you men to hear is
this. Jesus can rid you of crippling sin. That's why He
came among us. Look what sin has brought you to! Look
at the condition you're in! D'you think Almighty God
meant you to go through life like a hunted rat? Of course
He didn't. You fellows will never be able to escape Christ's
invitation to you. He says, "Come." That's it. He doesn't
care what kind of clothes you're wearing, whether your
years are thirty or seventy. All He asks is—are you heavy-
laden? Sin and its consequences make the heaviest burden
that anyone can carry. You say you've tried everything
you know to get rid of your burden. Have you tried Jesus?
What about giving Him a trial in your life?"

A very simple, straightforward talk understood by those
men. A stilted discourse full of long words and roundly
polished sentences would have just bored them to annoyance and revulsion. We sang—"What a Friend we have in
Jesus", then some Christian testimonies were given. As
witness after witness got up and told in calm tones how
their lives had been changed from sin and sorrow to joy in

Christ the Lord, I watched my ex-medical friend closely. Undoubtedly, he was visibly impressed. Some of the converts recounted his life story in many details through their own lives. They too, had missed the mark of their high calling, had experienced mind and heart bitterness, personal weaknesses, social failings. But what was clearly evident was that each and all radiated joy and confidence in God. They were completely changed in character, intention and ambition by absolute surrender to Christ's will. Then we sang the hymn.

> *Have Thine own way, Lord, Have Thine own way.*
> *Thou art the Potter, I am the clay.*
> *Mould me and make me after Thy will,*
> *While I am waiting, yielded and still.*

I was not one bit surprised that among the converts that night was ex-medical doctor Clifford M—. He came forward with noticeable eagerness evidently realising that for him it was a supreme question of life or death, now or never. Friends took charge of him.

In the morning he came to see me. What a mental and physical change there was in him. Gone the sullen, hang-dog expression, gone the attitude of hopelessness and despair, gone the trembling of his hands and limbs. Now he was bright-eyed, confident, radiant, alert. A new personality had taken over his old nature. After a meal and a prayer he joyfully shared with me his Christian testimony.

"As I knelt at the altar rail," he said, "I tried to pour out my whole heart to God, all my many sins and colossal failures. Then I seemed to expand in consciousness of God's life coming into mine. It was like a wave of tingling electricity sweeping through my body. I knew a life change had come. Jesus Christ seemed suddenly to step into my life and all was light and peace. I was strongly aware of an inner revolution bringing me unutterable happiness. I knew that I was converted, that Christ was my Saviour. An amazing mental and spiritual experience!"

In a busy hospital in San Francisco today there is a Christian man who, because of his medical knowledge, is often allowed to dispense medicine as well as to help staff doctors in sundry hospital duties. Due to his fine Christian character and influence he is greatly respected and admired. He is my old friend Cliff, once a very skilled surgeon and also a debauched hopeless outcast who waylaid me in a city street and badgered me for a morsel of food. Jesus Christ has now made a thorough good job of him.

Weary folks who pass him in the street
See Christ's love beam from out his wistful eyes.
And stake new confidence in God and man.

Chapter 9

Jesus said: "I Am the Resurrection and the Life."

THE *Greyhound* coach on which I was travelling stopped at Springfield, a large and thriving city in the American State of Massachusetts. Having a rest period of forty-five minutes, I wandered along one of the main streets greatly interested in the picturesque scene before me—the throbbing stream of road traffic, the restless crowd of men and women who closely brushed by me on the pavement, the constantly changing traffic lights and the winking many-coloured tradesmen's signs.

My attention was called to a number of men gazing through a dingy bookshop window. The stacked shelves inside were filled with brazen sexy American magazines, lurid, intimate pictures of semi-naked women, the kind of portraits deliberately and expressly published to excite the emotions and passions of men and to encourage them to purchase the glamorous periodicals. These promiscuous, falsely-named "art" books and risque "classics" do an enormous amount of harm to the minds and souls of vast hordes of our young folk, both male and female. It is, I am certain, outrageously wrong for the law to allow such literature.

I thought instantly of the goggle-eyed men and the sensual literature they were looking at soon after my American visitor began to talk to me. It was in the study of a ministerial acquaintance whose home I shared during my exchange ministry in Springfield's neighbouring state town of Northampton.

The friendly editor of the local *Northampton News* had opened his columns to me so that I was able to write a series of articles on many subjects. One on "The Dynamic Power of the Christian Faith" brought me many letters and several callers of different kinds. One of these faced me now.

One of the marks of the Christian minister is to suffer fools gladly. Like St. Paul of old, he has to be all things to all men that he might win some. I had a few visitors who considered that I had come from England solely to listen to their hard-luck stories, their whining appeals for money and their glib and foolish fables. But the large majority of my callers were intelligent, seriously-minded individuals who, because of the heavy demands and afflictions that life made upon them, felt compelled to seek counsel and support from one whom they considered was able and willing to give it. Among these was my new visitor who, from our first meeting, I felt strongly drawn to, and who is the subject of this story.

As he came up the pathway to my door, I could see that daily existence had lost all its zest and appeal for him. His step was a clumsy shuffle, his shoulders sagged heavily, his head veered from side to side as if he had lost all power to hold it still. He had all the marks of a sick and beaten man. I greeted him pleasantly and showed him to my study.

"Well my friend, how are you and what can I do for you?"

I was anxious for him to feel he was a welcome visitor to my temporary home and that I was ready to help him in any reasonable way. It must be very painful and humiliating for an individual to go and see the parson about some pressing personal problem or some aspect of God's work, only for him to feel that the cleric was not very interested and wanted to get rid of him as soon as possible. I believe that the primary qualification for a pastoral counsellor is his capacity to listen carefully to what others seek to tell him about their strains and troubles.

My visitor slumped into the armchair that I motioned him to. As I sat opposite he regarded me with a mingled look of suspicion and hostility. I noticed that his large head was framed on a thick neck, with a roll of flesh protruding over his white collar. His hair was touched with grey which thinned across his domed forehead. Dark shadows seamed under his slate-grey eyes. He jerked his hands to and fro as if they irritated him. Then he closed his eyes and a low moan escaped his lips. I waited for him to speak. Suddenly he blurted out:

"I'm done!"

"Done?" I asked. "How do you mean?"

It was a few seconds before he answered. He slowly raised his eyes. There was not a glint of brightness or hope in them.

"I'm finished, at the end of my tether. Nothing can be done for me." The words rapidly gushed from him.

"That isn't true," I answered gently. "You evidently feel that something can be done for you or else you wouldn't have come here to see me. Now tell me what's troubling you."

Again, he remained quiet for several moments. As he did so he squeezed his body together and ducked his head as if trying to avoid an opponent's blow. Gradually he relaxed, inhaled a loud breath and stared savagely at me.

"It's my nerves," he hissed sharply. "Nerves I tell you. They're driving me to hell. My God! I'm worn to a frazzle. I can't go on. I can't fight any longer. I'm a wreck. I've tried but it's no good. I'll have to quit. I'm finished, done for. That's all. Sorry to trouble you. I'll be going."

Not for the first time had I had in my study a man whose severe agony of mind had brought him nigh to the verge of self-destruction. I had no need to be an expert in human personality to sense that. My visitor was in the strong grip of mental evil forces. His nerves were shot to pieces. His whole body was suffering from complete inner disharmony.

I rose from my seat, stepped across to him and patted him on the shoulders.

"Look at me, friend! You're not finished you know. There's plenty of years left for you. For the moment you're very sick, sick chiefly in mind. And that sickness can be cured. I'm telling you the truth. I've seen it done, up and down this country and also in this very room. How about that? Somebody is going to get strength and courage to fight his fears. And that somebody, through the working power and grace of Almighty God, is going to win through. That somebody is you. Believe me, friend, I know what I'm talking about. If you will promise me to do your part, I tell you frankly and confidently, my Lord will do His. I have His authority for saying that. Right, before we go any further, how about a cup of coffee?"

A wan smile creased his cheeks. He drank the coffee I brought him with evident relish. As he sank back again within the arms of the chair he nodded to me, then his eyes searched the carpet as if seeking to focus on some object. He screwed up his face so tightly that it became a mass of fleshy ruts. I felt it necessary to get him talking.

"You're feeling better I hope for that coffee," I said. "Now, will you allow me to be your closest friend? Tell me anything and everything you like and I will promise to help you in any way I can to regain your health. It will do you a lot of good to unburden yourself, to share your troubles with someone else. So go ahead. Let's say we'll lick these infernal enemies of yours yet, whatever kind or shape they are. Ready? I'm listening."

Two or three times he opened his mouth as if fumbling for words. His eyes closed then he gave an audible little grunt.

"Right," he said with an effort. "Here goes! I don't think you'll like what I'm going to say. Don't be afraid to stop me if you can't take it. For God's sake be honest with me! If you can't do anything for me, then say so!"

He came to a sudden halt and heavily beetled his brows. Another long period of silence followed.

"You haven't said much yet," I remarked. "Come on, make an effort. Trust me to help you if I can."

He gazed wildly at me then started again to convulse his body in various motions, left to right, forward and backward. My eyesight wasn't improved by watching him. He was behaving in a crazy fashion. Gradually, he ceased his physical motions, stroked his face, then riveted his eyes once more on me. An explosive burst of words suddenly poured from his mouth.

"I'm rotten, I tell you. I'm a sex pervert, a vice monger, a homosexual, a depraved low-down rotter. That's what I am. And—I've come here to see you. I'm not fit to be here. Why don't you boot me out! Look at me? Look what I've come to? I'm a physical wreck. My nerves are all in a tangle. They've got me beat. I can't act sensibly. I can't sleep. I've got hideous vermin crawling all over my mind. All sorts of horrible sprites gibber at me when I try to pull myself together. They hack and cut me about as if they love to see me bleeding in every part of me. Mister, it's terrible. I feel I will go out of my mind if it doesn't stop. I've been near to doing away with myself many times. It's all because I'm a debauched idiot, because I've been a willing slave to my passions for many years. My God, what shall I do?"

His staccato sentences streamed from him like a flood then finished abruptly. He wiped his eyes where tears had gathered, thence continued to glare in my direction.

"Don't stop me," he said loudly. "I must confess, get it off my chest. Where was I? Oh, I know! I was telling you about my evil habits, wasn't I? Man, they've put a strong net about me. I'm bound I tell you, bound in body and mind. You talk about d-t's! What is it—*delirium tremens*? I know those experiences. I haven't been in the drunkard's 'Inferno' but I have been in the sex-maniac's 'Inferno'. And I believe that's worse than the other. Funny thing, or is it funny, I'm not a drunkard and never have been. I detest alcohol. Can't stand the smell of it. I don't go round the pubs. My drink is chiefly coffee. I'm not mastered by beer like crowds of others, but I am by sex. For years it's been all sex with me. I've worshipped it. Started when I was a boy. Those so-called art pictures, those sexy pin-ups. I used to stick them all round the walls of my bedroom. Of course, look at the bad influence they had on my young mind! I was surrounded with them day and night. You're a parson. You know about that text in the Bible that says you can't gather grapes from thorns, don't you? Of course you can't! You see, I grew up to indulge my sexual appetite. Thought I was big and smart. I couldn't see anything pure and reverent in women. All I thought about them was that they were sex companions, just there to satisfy my bodily desires. Look at the harm I've done to them! Look what I've bequeathed to them! Impurity, lack of self-control, inflamed passions and no mite of respect! My, what a depraved rotter I am? I know I'm not fit to live. Those art pictures, obscene novels— they're plain incitements for lust and that's what they're published for. And I was a sucker, egged on by these lewd things. Couldn't control myself. No woman was safe with me. I went on and on until my passions arranged with my nerves to bring me down. And what a fall? Look at me now! My jumpy body, my watery eyes, my restless hands, my jangled nerves! What a mess I'm in! Jolly near death, mister. I mean Reverend. Ruined by self-dissipation. That's me!"

He stopped to clear his throat and again to wipe his eyes. He looked the picture of complete misery. It was easy to see that he was strongly enslaved by the powerful physical vice of lust. Watching him, I recalled the man mentioned in St. Mark's Gospel who was possessed with a devil. The record says that this inner fiend bound him with fetters and chains and left him "as one dead". My companion was a modern counterpart of this Biblical character. His life too had become a grievous hell of suffering and remorse. He straightened his bent and swaying body and began talking again. Now that he had removed the barrier before his tongue he seemed desperately anxious to continue to confide in me.

"Do you know," he went on, "that I do really want to be and to do good. I do want to be straight and decent. I hate myself that my rotten sexual habits are stopping me being what I truly ache to be, a man of high character, in love with the sacred and beautiful. Oh yes, there is that side of me. I'm very glad of it. But the evil in me is stronger than the good. I'm so weak willed . . . Reverend, I'm feeling a bit better now that I've opened up to you. I saw your last *News* article and felt that I had to come and see you. I know you've had a wide experience of men, seen a lot of fellows just like me. I'm sure of this, they couldn't have been as bad as I am. Anyhow, I'm willing to follow your advice. If you can only help me, help me to break these sinful habits of mine, I'll do anything you say. All I know is I must beat this sex demon, recover my nerve and look every person straight in the face. I must if I'm going to keep sane."

He gave a deep sigh of relief and literally flung himself back in his chair.

"Thank you, friend, for your candour and your confidence in me," I said. "I, too, am glad you came here. I told you I would help you if I possibly could. I'm sure I can do that. I'm a parson as you know. Let me add a further word. I am also happy to be a Christian man. I say that because some people declare that many parsons are not Christians. Maybe they're right. For many years I've tried to be a Christian in word and deed. I've stumbled quite a lot I know, let down my Lord a good number of times. But I've gone to Him quickly and expressed my regret and asked for strength to do better in the future. You see, I've got enough brains to know that if more people became Christians it would be better for them and for this old world. That's plain, day-to-day common sense. My friend, never regard Christianity as something that's just bound up with the Church—you know, Sunday worship, Bible reading and hymn singing. Unfortunately, many folk do just look upon it as that and nothing more. They tend to shut up Jesus Christ in the church after the Sunday services and leave Him there till the following Sunday. That won't do. The Christianity of Christ is a positive, sure, mental, moral and spiritual Power that can be applied to every department of our personal, national and international life. It's with us to-day, a practical, certain remedy for all the sicknesses that plague and distress us. If people everywhere pledged themselves to ascertain and follow the mind of Christ in every avenue of their lives, of a truth there would be a revolution for the public good. Can't you see that?"

My companion eyed me with keen interest and slowly nodded his head.

"Take your case!" I went on. "I could accompany you to a psychologist, a doctor, a welfare officer. But honestly, I don't believe these are the gentry who could cure you of your present ailment. I'm convinced, that like myriads more, your big trouble is spiritual. You need a thorough clean-up inside. Once your mind is steeped in things of nobility and godliness, once you are willing to allow Christ to have a say in your life, I'm as sure as I sit here that the transformation in your life and condition will be certain and beautiful to behold. I stand by that firm statement."

"I believe you've got something," he said simply.

We had a word of prayer together and I arranged for him to return to me the following week. Before he left I asked him to promise me on his honour that during the intervening days he would not indulge in any sexual act with either men or women, that he would not read any lewd novels or go to a town night club. He promised me solemnly that he would not do any of these things.

On the day arranged he was back in my study. How glad I was to notice that the previous coils of oppressive melancholy which then had wrapped themselves tightly around him, were now absent. There was a new spring in his steps, fresh brightness in his eyes, some colour in his cheeks. I felt that the fire of renewed confidence was beginning to burn again in his heart. He shook hands firmly with me.

"I've done it," he said brightly. "A whole week without lust of any kind. And I'm feeling better too."

The oncoming months cemented a close friendship between us. I gathered from his frequent talks with me that at his High School he had been initiated in the habit of self-abuse by other boys and that this practice had taken a firm hold on him in his successive years. His parents

were Methodists and he went regularly to church until
he was twenty years of age. Then he married a girl of
eighteen, quickly had two children, and owing to his per-
verted acts and unreasonable marital demands, his wife
left him taking the two bairns with her. He then formed
adulterous associations with various women, committed
constant homosexual acts with men of his corrupt kind,
and, in consequence, played havoc with his body until he
was reduced to a nervous wreck. With difficulty, he main-
tained his job in the office of a local dry goods store only
through the goodness of his manager, who, knowing much
about him, warned him repeatedly about his sordid way
of life. Middle-aged, in lodgings owing to his own folly,
his sinful offences catching up with him after thirty years,
bereft of true love and friendship, thinking often about
making an end of his useless, self-indulgent life, he came
to me. With mounting pity I listened to his sorrowful
story of personal failure, domestic chaos and tragic ill-
health.

Open confession, it is said, is good for the soul. "Confess
your faults one to another," the Scripture counsels us.
There can be no healthier procedure providing the people
concerned in the confession are sincere and upright, fully
desiring each other's total welfare. My friend James, as
I came to know him, seized every opportunity when he sat
with me in my study, to eliminate and cleanse his mind of
the deep-seated poison that for far too long he had imbibed,
by opening all avenues into his innermost life and by frank
and full acknowledgement of his heinous, hated sins. As
a result, this act brought great relief to him and, as the
weeks passed, he benefited by a distinct and noticeable
return to health.

At our every meeting I talked to him about the wisdom
and urgency of allowing Christ to manage his life. Rapidly

he was regaining his lost manhood and taking increased interest in our religious discussions.

"James," I said to him one evening, "God is not content to allow a prodigal son like you to continue to dwell in the far country. I think you understand what I mean. Why don't you return home to Him? Why don't you acknowledge that Jesus Christ is not only a world Physician but also a universal and a personal Saviour. Yours and mine. That's the greatest truth confronting us all. You, I'm sure, do know His record and mission. He comes among us to change the pattern of individual life for good. He can change a criminal into a saint. He can take a twisted personality like yours and transform it into one of superb beauty and honour. Why not let Him take over?"

I was sure that the work of grace was proceeding daily in his heart. On Friday evenings I held a devotional meeting in the home. A dozen or so people crammed into it. One evening, without any prompting, James joined us. Glancing at him during the proceedings, I sensed that he was greatly impressed with the speakers and their testimonies. They did not attempt to push God down the throats of others who were present. Simply and quietly they told of what Christ meant to them, the radical change that had come over their lives since they pledged their allegiance to Him. James seldom missed his group meeting after that.

A few weeks elapsed and one memorable night, a speaker at the meeting, a man who had had a corrupt past, told us that because of his total surrender to Christ, life had taken on a new valuation. It had completely changed in content, aim and purpose. He had now found peace and joy in believing, following and serving his new and adored Master. We waited a few seconds for the next speaker. To my unbounded delight, James slowly got to his feet. His face was tense with emotion. He cleared his throat and inhaled a deep breath. His brief testimony was electric with revelation and sincerity. He abandoned himself to his heart-pulsing message. It was the liberating outpouring of a sensitive, self-condemned soul. He relentlessly chastised himself for his insensate folly. There were no self-excuses or half-concealments. Frankly, softly, he made a clean breast of his many sins over the past years, his mental and physical torture, his thoughts of suicide and his call on me.

"I look along the way that I've come," he concluded, "and I'm sorry to tell you that for a very long time I've been the devil's willing slave. Now I mean to be God's eager servant. I want to learn of Him. Now that I've told you, my friends, much about myself, please, please pray for me. From this night I go forward to serve Him until my earthly journey is finished!"

His moving testimony just flooded the souls of his hearers with reverence and thankfulness. No one else spoke that night. Everybody present was too full with emotion to say anything. We all felt that we had entered the highest heaven. A sweet, pervasive sense of peace, holiness, rest and blessedness nestled deeply in every heart.

From that time forward my friend James became a moral and spiritual giant. Revealingly, God was the harmonising factor of his life. He showed himself daily in his thoughts, words and deeds to be God-possessed. His old life of sensuality slipped from him like a freely discarded garment. It became as natural for him to talk about his new Christian faith as another man talks about his pet hobbies. Everything he touched, his work, his reading, his shop colleagues, his writing—all were now linked with God's presence in his daily life. The kinship with his Lord was plain to see by any intelligent observer. His sole desire was to:

Follow with reverent steps the great example
Of Him whose holy task was doing good.

One evening, he turned up unexpectedly at my temporary home. He brought with him a heavy suitcase.

"I had to come," he said smilingly. "I've brought the old devil's wares with me. Being in lodgings, I couldn't burn them in the boiler. Could I please make a big bonfire of them at the bottom of the garden?" There, he emptied the case of a big pile of lurid, sexy English and American magazines, obscene books and nude photographs of men and women."

"Look," he said pertinently, "my daily portion of poisonous food for many years. I fed my mind, brain and soul with that unhealthy sewage literature. D'you wonder that I became an over-sexed human animal, nearly lost all my brains, and thought of doing away with myself?"

I poured some paraffin on the big heap of sordid print and soon reduced it to red-hot ashes. Both of us went into supper feeling satisfied that we had done our profitable good deed for the day.

During the remaining time of my American pastorate, James became my close confidante and friend. His face reflected a Christ-like look. An inner light shone from it and an impressive nobility emanated from his whole being. I knew that he had received the blest ordination of the pierced hands. Observing him constantly and greatly strengthened by the force of his Christian character, I was gratefully conscious that I was in the presence of a wondrous miracle, the miracle performed by my beloved Lord, the miracle of a transformed and Christ-revealing quality of life.

The goodbye was not easily said. In our prayer fellowship we ardently committed each other into the safe hands of our Father-God.

"Reverend," he said softly, looking at me with a face that shone, "my sights are now focused on higher things and no longer on things of the gutter. I know now the meaning of His heartening words—'I am the resurrection and the life.' I've been resurrected, you know. My Lord and my God!"

As the road coach travelled rapidly in the direction of New York, I thought much about the congregation of "down-and-outs" which I would soon be addressing in the renowned Bowery Mission of New York, very many of them abject sex slaves like my dear comrade James used to be. I would eagerly tell them of the divine power which first controlled his sex appetite, then powerfully and effectively eliminated it wholly. Then I would plead with them to allow me to introduce them to One who could, if only they would let Him do so, free them from the bondage of their fleshly lusts and lead them into the glorious liberty of the children of God.

I thought too, of the devoted, Christ-enthused Mission Superintendent, a big sinner saved by grace, a much-scorched human brand saved from burning, whose very colourful life I write about in the next chapter.

Chapter 10

JESUS SAID: "I CAME TO SEEK AND SAVE."

B EING thoroughly human, there are times in my life
when I feel the explosive force of righteous indigna-
tion within me. At those times I want to express
both my anger and my anguish in strong, pungent words.
I feel like that when I see printed lies in newspaper adver-
tisements and on roadside hoardings. "Beer is best",
"Whisky is good for you". Whenever I read those blatant
untruths I think of the increasing list of road accidents, of
maimed lives, of shocking deaths, caused in many cases
by drunken motor-car and lorry drivers. I recall the number of people I have been asked to bury, people who despite
the tactful cause of death inserted on the death certificate,
truly died of alcoholic poisoning. I recollect the teeming
hordes of men I have met, lived, slept and ate with in men's
hostels, lodging houses and rescue missions, men dirty,
foul, debased, whom I have ministered to, had in my own
home-hostel for many weeks, men utterly broken in body
and mind, penniless, workless, hopeless, the great majority
of them brought down to their sad, gutterish condition
by one destroying, hellish agency—plainly and undeniably,
intoxicating alcoholic liquor. I think too of my trusty
friend Raymond Allen whose tangled life has been a saga
of unforgettable, contradictory experiences.

For nearly twenty-five years Ray was an ardent devil's
disciple. All the corrupt, enfeebling vices placed at his

disposal by his exulting, knavish master were eagerly accepted and readily sampled. He has known riches and poverty, pleasure and pain, success and destitution, freedom and bondage. Little wonder that as he talks, anger and anguish will vigorously force his words as he refers to his sin-saturated days. Then, as he recounts how he found the way out of his deep Slough of Despond, how unexpectedly he met the Saviour Who miraculously re-created his whole personality, his eyes and face flash a glistening light of wonder and praise. He is a most winsome personality and his smile takes the chill from a dull day. To look at him no person of average intelligence would suspect that like the Prodigal Son, he had been in the far country of degrada-tion and want, and too, like the Prodigal, that there came to him sordid, pain-filled moments when he would have gladly filled his empty stomach with the scraps that the swine did eat.

Ray is an American born into a large family in the Southern State of Minnesota. They were desperately poor and his father was constantly sick. After his death, life became a turmoil of worry and a scramble for bread. Ray's mother was compelled to take in washing and sew for her neighbours. The boys were sent out to do odd jobs in the neighbourhood and Ray, though small, could always be relied on to augment the family purse by performing heavy labouring tasks that any intelligent man present would have stopped him doing. His parents were good Christians and religion was in the air he breathed. He accepted it casually and as he grew older came to consider it uninviting, milk-and-water stuff. He became tired of poor-relief meals and free hand-outs of clothing by chari-table organisations and decided at the age of thirteen to leave school and find full-time employment. Was not his pair of long trousers which now he proudly wore the evident symbol of his strong, vigorous manhood? Couldn't he fight successfully any local boy of his own size—and often bigger? And why have any contact with sour-faced "goody-goodies" who didn't seem to enjoy the religion they often prated about? Not for him Church life. It was boringly dull. All church folk seemed to live in an ancient, dry-as-dust world. He had no inclination to join them nor was he in any way influenced by what they said or what they stood for.

He tried several local jobs, joined a gang of teen-age toughs, found it the accepted custom to use foul swear words and drink a cheap heady wine called "Sneaky Pete". By the time he was sixteen he was habitually guzzling "sneaky".

"All my pals were drinking it," he said, his broad forehead creased with annoyance and shame, "so why shouldn't I? Boozing was the badge of our so-called friendship. At first I used to worry about its ill effect on me, and also, I didn't like the taste of it. But I got used to it and could soon drink with the best of them. As young as I was, I got fired from many jobs because I took time off to go and get a liquor bottle from the nearest saloon. When my middle-aged mother found out the way I was living her hair turned grey with worry within a few months."

Ray eventually came to the place where his youthful folly began to taunt and upbraid him. He was unemployed, he borrowed money from members of his ne'er-do-well team but showed no anxiety to repay them. He offended respectable people because he couldn't express himself without profanity. He found himself in a difficult school which was famed for its hard knocks. Causing trouble in many ways through his desire for a self-indulgent life, he thought it time to seek pastures new. He ran away from home, left a widowed mother in the agony of despair and went off to see what kind of a world it was outside the borders of his small home town.

It was all right at first. He didn't get into too much trouble. But he gained speed and unpleasant knowledge as he roamed along. From State to State he went. He worked at odd jobs. When he had money he slept in flophouses and men's hostels. When he hadn't, any filthy doorway, basement, shed, would do. Mostly he was hungry, dirty, wet and cold. Whenever he could hide away he rode freight trains. The paramount thought in his mind was the liquor bottle, and often with a little money in his possession he indulged in a drunken spree. Sometimes he tried to stop his drinking but after one sip of the intoxicant he had to finish the remainder in a very short time.

World War One broke out and he enlisted in the United States Navy. Now he could satisfy his thirst for liquor to the full. Money was regular and plentiful. He was eager to prove that he could take his drinking and gambling with the toughest members of the crew. At the ship's bar there was liquor much stronger than cheap wine. He developed a specialised taste for whisky. It made him feel manly and confident—for a time. Sometimes he found himself on a charge for neglect of duties because his drunken condition caused him to stay in bed too long. At each port of call the waterfront saloon was his welcome nursery. Often he drank himself into unconsciousness, and after his mates had carried him back to the ship, he awoke hours afterwards to discover that his wallet had gone and his pockets were empty.

The war over he signed as a merchant seaman on an American freighter. Visiting most countries in the world he became more and more enslaved in the bondage of drunkenness. After his discharge, deadening, aimless drifting became his everyday life. Sometimes there turned up a job as when by a stroke of luck he was able to enter the insurance business. Money came in; it departed more quickly. He drank up most of what he earned. Being a good cook at sea, he borrowed some cash to start a dining house. In a very short time the bartender in a nearby saloon found he had a good customer in Ray. Inevitably the financial crash came and once more he found himself a homeless, penniless foot-slogger of the road. Having served customers at tables filled with an abundance of food, Ray now found himself very often looking under the lid of a garbage bin for something to eat.

His situation became desperate. He had no home, no friends, no work. His clothes were dirty and threadbare. He was haggard in appearance, looking and feeling wearily old. Objectless and hopeless, he staggered along, painful starvation causing his steps to become increasingly weaker. There came a day when he couldn't go any further. He woke up in a hospital ward. Satiated with good food, rest and nursing attention he rapidly got better and sensibly surveyed his future days.

"I will make good," he vowed, gritting his teeth in desperation. "I'll beat the booze yet, get a good job and have a nice home of my own yet. You'll see!"

He looked round at his hospital mates with eyes of glad satisfaction, cheered by his comforting resolution. A Christian visitor, showing personal interest in him, gave him a couple of dollars for a future rainy day. That and a few dimes he had earned doing odd jobs for the nursing staff soon went when, once more a free man, he sat on the high stool in a down-town saloon drinking a cheap heady bottle of "Pink Lady". He had not sufficient moral stamina to keep straight. He begged his food, slept rough at nights in sheds, fields or empty houses and drank all he could get hold of to drown his sorrows. Lurching hand in hand with the devil he tottered feebly towards the abyss.

Three more years passed. He was still a social pariah. Painfully dragging his feet, his stomach one aching vacuum, his odorous clothes rotting away on him, he stumbled into the city of Albany, in New York State, one early evening. A well-dressed man loomed in front of him. Desperation and the urgency of physical needs caused Ray to ask him for monetary assistance.

"See that badge, bud?" the man replied brusquely, revealing the metal token of a policeman under his coat lapel. "I'm a plain-clothes cop so you've asked the wrong feller, haven't you? I could nab you for begging, you know. See my mate in uniform over there! He's a Christian. You talk to him."

"Well, what's the trouble?" asked the uniformed officer, when Ray stood meekly in front of him. "You don't look too good."

Ray replied that he was starving and asked where he could get a little food.

"Seems to me," said the policeman in a kindly tone, "that you need both food for your body and for your soul. Get me? Look, go down there, first turning to your right, and you'll find a Rescue Mission. That's what you want. You'll get the right kind of food there. Make you a new man. Good luck!"

Ray ambled away thoroughly annoyed. Food for the soul! He wanted no pious blurb about "being saved". He turned down a side street. Many years had passed since he set foot in a church of any kind. He knew nothing of missions, of their superb redemptive, emancipating work. He sauntered on, losing himself in a maze of side alleys. Too late he found himself again in the main street he had recently left. The policeman beckoned to him in a peremptory manner.

"So you gave the mission a miss, did you? All right. Here's the choice! You're a vagrant and I can take you in for that. Also you've been begging. That's another charge. So what is it to be? The mission where they'll do you good, or a spell in jail? What about it?"

Ray shifted uneasily. He wanted to get out of the sight of the cop. He drifted away and turned into another street. To his surprise and annoyance his eyes caught sight of a large metal sign hung prominently over a shabby doorway. The electric light blazed conspicuously the two words —"Jesus Saves." Then in large letters on the window he read: "Albany Rescue Mission."

He shook his head derisively. "Not for me," he mumbled. "For kids and women, that's all."

Then he looked down and caught sight of his shabby clothes, his cracked boots. He ran a rough hand over his stubbly beard. He was desperately hungry and tired. Nobody cared, nobody wanted him. What was there to live for? From the interior of the mission came the sound of singing. It sounded pleasant to him. Almost unthinkingly he pushed open the door and went in. Finding a seat about half-way down, he glanced uneasily about him. The building was plain and unprepossessing with rows of forms both sides of the aisle. The congregation consisted mostly of ill-dressed men like himself. The man on the platform had a kindly face and led the singing with enthusiasm. The hymns they sang Ray had never heard before, but their jingling tunes made him feel better.

The leader began to speak and Ray settled himself for a much-needed nap. In his sub-conscious mind he suddenly heard the familiar words "drink" and "dope". He opened his eyes and concentrated his attention on the speaker.

"Like some of you, my brothers, for many years I was a plain, booze-soaked fool. I drank away some precious years of my life, years that I would like to have back again to re-use for more worthy ends. I lost everything that a real man wants in this life, my home, my family, my work and my self-respect. I thought of ending it all, the rotten coward that I was. Then one unforgettable day, alone and friendless, I passed a church which was open. I hadn't been in one for years yet I felt compelled to go into that one. I don't mind telling you that I had a good sleep. When I woke up I saw a Bible on the shelf in front of me. I turned over a few pages then I found myself reading the words of Jesus—'Come unto Me all ye that labour and are heavy laden and I will give you rest'. All at once something seemed to happen inside me. I felt those words were addressed to me. Somehow I knew it. I clenched my dirty fists upward and pleaded with Christ to do something for me. I remember praying something like this—'Dear Jesus Christ, you've got to listen to me. I'm all wrong and twisted and het up. I'm a rotter and not fit to talk to you. I've drunk away the best years of my life and now I'm just sick of it, sick of everything. I want to be different. I want You. Please take me over. I'm whipped.'

"Men, believe it or not, I walked out of that church a new man. I felt different. Jesus said, 'Come', so I came. I mean, I suddenly knew that God loved me in spite of everything and could, if I let Him, make a decent job of me. So I asked Him to do it. That's conversion. That's the Christian message. What He did for me He can do for you. Who's going to give Him the chance tonight?"

Ray Allen sat spellbound. He felt that what the preacher was saying had a definite meaning for him, that what he was offering was just what he most needed. It made common sense to him. His past life had brought him unhappiness, ill-health, wretchedness. He had no work, money or home. His clothes were patched and threadbare, his body was pinched with hunger, his face sallow and unwashed. All because he had had no Christ in his life and been the devil's fool. Well, according to the preacher he could alter all that. The congregation began to sing:

> *I am coming, Lord,*
> *Coming now to Thee,*
> *Wash me, cleanse me in the blood*
> *That flowed on Calvary.*

The leader then prayed for prodigals, for those who had many chances and by their folly neglected to use them well. He asked that as a result of that service many in that hall might grip the hand of Jesus and know the joy of forgiveness, peace and newness of life.

For a short time Ray felt the Spirit of God wrestling with his inner self. He felt he wanted to end the old life; he wanted to be clean and decent, to be a real and true man, not a poor apology of one. Yes, why not be a Christian, offer his life completely to Jesus Christ? Suddenly he knew he was saying goodbye to crippling sin, to squalid saloon bars and cheap heady liquor, to a life of dreary vagabondage. He got to his feet and walked boldly and eagerly to the altar rail and there offered himself unreservedly to His Saviour.

That was nearly *twenty-five years* ago. Throughout the passing years he has increasingly widened his vision of the redeeming Christ and the wide world's need. He has entered into a religious experience which has lifted him into a new range of spiritual consciousness. Life now for him thrills with divine vitality and is radiant with purpose and service. The all-pervading Presence of his loved Master has brought a dedicated love of vocation and of power, a constant yearning compassion for Christless souls.

If ever you are in the unsavoury district of the Bowery in New York City, where at any time of the day you can see a pathetic collection of human wrecks meandering aimlessly up and down the dirty pavements, call in and see the smiling radiant *new Superintendent of the world-famous Bowery Mission.* His name is the Rev. Raymond Allen, once a drunken outcast, now God's consecrated minister to the human dregs of society. As daily they come within the orbit of his mission ministry he pleads with them to follow his example, make Christ Jesus their eager Guest, Friend and Saviour.

Chapter 11

AN increasing number of people the world over are complaining of weariness and nervous tension. They confess to feeling the strain of life. They own to being baffled and defeated. The exacting routine of customary tasks, the daily duties of the common round, the vexing frets and fears caused by the general anarchy and unrest in the universe, are sapping their mental and physical strength. Such are the facts reported by publicists, investigators, writers and physicians.

They accord with my findings as I travel the globe conducting services and missions in different countries. I have talked to many people who have sadly confessed that they have mechanically existed for a number of years yet never truly and purposefully lived. They are alive because their hearts are beating, yet they have never known how to live life. They know about many other things yet life, thrilling with superb meaning, mission and power, is a total stranger to them.

The ever-mounting financial millions being spent on universal health schemes is a measure of the world's mind, body and soul sickness. Hospitals are alarmingly overcrowded. Doctors and psychiatrists have an unending queue of patients. The list of mentally wrought people pathetically seeking help and guidance is a constantly growing one. Tranquillizing pills and drugs are being sold and dispensed in enormous quantities. My newspaper recently reported the story of a half-demented man who dashed into a city office shouting, "Who am I?" He looked under tables, pulled up a carpet, searched a cupboard and stared out of a window. When the police were summoned he was asked what he was searching for.

"I'm trying to find myself," he said frantically. So are myriads more. They are lost in the eddies of despair and futility. They are like some of my tramp friends; they wander to and fro on the earth, aimless, hopeless, purposeless.

Into our vocabulary has come a new word—escapism. More and more folk are seeking to get away from customary duties, responsibilities and realities. They attempt to escape into a dream world of drugs and drink and incessant amusement. They don't want much time to think. They want others to amuse them. In radio, television, drama and the film, they are far too often confronted with a very low standard of values which depicts sex as the chief aim and end of life and the valuable home-making virtues as old-fashioned and humdrum. Is it any wonder then that moral problems are increasingly besetting us, that our catalogue of crime lengthens continually, that figures for juvenile delinquency grow every year and that violence, thuggery and immorality are debauching the country!

There is so much bad behaviour in the world today that it is impossible to keep track of all of it. Our newspapers fall over themselves to publish, even on the front page, grubby stories of people who seem to glory in living sewerage lives. We are told much about the doings of people called film stars. If only these individuals truly and brightly twinkled in a beneficent, uplifting manner!

Let us face the issue squarely and honestly. The way

our country and the world is going at present is bound
to lead to tragic and abyssmal disaster. Far too many
people of evil report and practice are seeking to turn the
universe into a lazar house. Around us are many ugly
things that injure good eyesight and bemean ordinary
intelligence. Dereliction of duty, skimping of work, greedy
plotting for personal advantage, ceaseless and monotonous
emphasis on self, self, self. "All things are yours," is
the incessant cry. Everything belongs to you. "Glory
to man in the highest for man is the master of all
things."

That is the philosophy called Humanism. It is man
centred. It declares that man has within himself all the
resources he needs for his true welfare in this life. Why
worry about any other? Man has shown himself to be
very clever. The material world is his box of toys. His
material progress, scientific development and mechanical
efficiency stand at a higher point than at any other time
in human history. And yet, the world is full of unrest.
Materialism and the things of the physical plane have not
brought to human hearts either the peace or contentment
which the world so much desires and for which every
true heart ardently longs. The material world is glutted
with the things which a large number of people imagine
make for happiness, but happiness is an outstanding prize
which seems to escape them.

The old Biblical writer had a firm hand on the pulse of
truth when he said: "Except the Lord build the house
they labour in vain that build it." You cannot run a
world successfully without taking God into consideration
regarding human affairs. God is love and peace, and service
and brotherhood; you cannot rest the well-being of eternal
souls upon the things which perish. Life at its best and
highest must always be centred in Him Who is the human

expression of God. God, for priceless love of us, actually clothed Himself in our very flesh and blood, offering us in Christ a new and satisfying kind of life. There is no sure way to peace, no other way to a just and happy society, no other way to right relationships between man and man, than the plain and certain way of God through Jesus Christ.

Recently the British Transport Commission banned the placing of Bibles in railway hotels owned by them. In the high name of righteousness and common sense—why? When asked the reason for this nonsensical action the answer given was that it would not be in the best interests of their guests. The Holy Bible, the outstanding Book of truth and wisdom in the world, the Book that sets forth the high moral standards of life and character that made our Empire and country truly great, the Book that stresses the priceless virtues of goodness, honesty, purity and love as necessary ingredients which make for uprightness and happiness! The Bible banned for tired and travel-stained travellers. Amazing! Had it been Tom Paine's *Age of Reason* or Hitler's *Mein Kampf* one could have understood it. Many sensible people will affirm that the more the Bible is read in hotels of all types the likelihood is that fewer "souvenirs" in the form of cutlery and crockery would be taken away.

Why do we go on committing moral and spiritual suicide in this very foolish manner! Judges and magistrates constantly proclaim their concern that far too many people are calling evil good, sin antiquated and impurity right and natural. It is not enough to teach our young folk in schools the lessons of science, technology and the arts. Above all they need to be taught more about the meaning and practice of the Christian religion, if they are going to develop into worthy, God-fearing citizens.

They tell me the story of Jesus is old,
    And they ask that we teach something new,
They say that the Babe, and the Man of the Cross,
    For the wise of this world will not do.

But what can we say to the seeking heart,
    If we preach not salvation from sin,
And how can we comfort the souls that depart,
    If we tell not that Christ rose again?

Ponder that term "salvation". Why has that royal, pregnant word for far too many people been allowed to slip into the hushed by-lanes of their vocabulary as if it stood for something very secret or unimportant? It is the sovereign word of the Christian faith. It is the universal message of the Christian Church. It is the exhilarating Gospel of Good News that proclaims the wonder and glory of the Christian evangel. It explains why Jesus came among us. It is the complete and convincing answer to man's hunger after a Presence and a Power which satisfies his deepest needs. It is the astounding miracle which assures man that he is no stray atom in a wondrous universe but an erring yet well-loved child of God. Salvation is the joyous turning of a man to God, the soul's conscious discovery of the Saviour. When men first confronted Him and heard Him calling them to a new order of life, they discovered that when they submitted their wills to His obedience, gave themselves to His cleansing power, they were lifted up to a new level and into a new understanding of life. They experienced the precious reality of Salvation.

Read avidly your New Testament and mark the lilting and descriptive phrases that refer to men and women who have moved out upon this new Christian way of living into this Christ-invested kind of life. "Born again," "born from above," "translated out of darkness into light," from the power of Satan unto God," "a new creation," "putting off the old and putting on the new man," "passing from death to life," "dying and rising again."

These Christ-owned people experienced a spiritual rebirth. As a result they gladly forsook their evil ways. The coming of Jesus to them was the cause of it. He stood in their midst. He entered their hearts. Confronted by Him they abdicated from their self-life in favour of His indwelling life. He did not come among them enclosed in convention, creed, ritual and superstition. He simply and lovingly said: "Follow Me." He offered them eagerly and freely that which would make the weak strong, the coward brave, the poor rich, the captives free. "There is nothing to pay," He said. "It is free for all." Jesus paid the price Himself. It cost Him the desolation of Gethsemane, the Crown of Thorns, the betrayal of treacherous men, the agony of Calvary.

Recently I looked upon the Kelvin Building in the Australian city of Adelaide. Lord Kelvin was one of the greatest physical scientists this world has ever known. On one occasion he was asked by a research student: "Excuse me, sir, what is the greatest discovery you have ever made?" This was Kelvin's answer: "The greatest discovery I ever made was the day when I realised that Jesus Christ was my Saviour and Lord."

Idle words? No! True words, wise words, words of hope and courage and power. "Blessed be the God and Father of our Lord Jesus Christ through whose mercy we have been born anew." "The love of Christ constrains us." Such has been the ennobling cry of countless hosts of men and women who have been genuinely and permanently changed by the transforming power of Jesus. Human nature can be radically changed by the advent of the Master into the life of the individual. I have seen Jesus at work all over the world, in the lives of people of all colours, ages and conditions. Those trapped in self-defeat have emerged victorious; the impure have become pure, the weak strong, the ungodly righteous.

Here is Matthew, the publican, the extortioner, the money-grabber. Probably held in great contempt by his fellow Jews because he worked for their Roman masters. He met Jesus, left his money-bags and followed the Lord on a new life of religious adventure. Here is Mary Magdalene, once pretty, now tarnished and corrupted by heinous deeds. Jesus gripped her soul, called her to be His disciple and she followed Him. Here is Simon, the blusterer, the erratic, the haughty. He is fortunate to encounter Jesus and in consequence he acquires new life, judgments, values and standards. "Thou art the Christ, the Son of the Living God," he exclaims after the Saviour has delivered Him from his spoiling sins. Saul the zealous persecutor of Christ becomes Paul the dedicated ambassador of Christ after he had been stopped by Jesus on the road. Augustine was a foul libertine. After his Lord had entered his life he became one of the greatest theologians and preachers in the then known world. Francis of Assisi, a gay playboy in his youth, surfeited by his father's riches, becomes an outstanding Christ-devoted disciple from the day the Master took over the management of his life. The Wesleys, the Bunyans, the Howards, the Booths, the Grenfells, the Barnados, the mighty host who followed them in the heavenly way, found themselves on top of life instead of underneath it after they had talked with Jesus and given themselves to Him.

No one can argue against a life that is Christ possessed. Many can and do argue against creeds and theologies and churches, but when a human soul is gripped by the

Saviour Christ and reveals inward peace and outward rapture then criticism is hushed and abandoned.

If Jesus reigned supremely in all men's hearts, would it be a better world? Should we have this fearful muddle and unrest in which the whole universe is seething? If only mankind from all quarters of the globe would be wise to heed the Saviour Christ, what He taught, what He lived and died for, what He could accomplish in their hearts and lives if they would but let Him; if only they would sample His transforming and redeeming power, what life, joy, mastery and victory would be theirs and what abiding peace, good will and brotherhood would flood the entire globe. It is the whole wide world for Jesus or else a vast, soulless, cosmic lunatic asylum.

We have a Gospel that is working miracles of redemption today. These challenging stories of men and women I successively met in Melbourne, Sydney, Auckland, Wellington, San Francisco, Chicago, New York and London, which are recorded here, wondrously illustrate that fact.

On my return to England I was soon confronted with the same problems that faced me everywhere I went abroad. The stark, calamitous problems of human folly, wretchedness, evil and degradation. They are not the copyright of one class or race of people. They burden the lives of black and white, of brown and yellow citizens. They are international. The positive, undeniable truth is that sin is a universal disease and that Jesus Christ is a universal Saviour. That is a stupendous, life-warming fact that no intelligent person can deny. From every nation under the sun people of all kinds and colours can make their way to Him and find rest of heart and peace of soul. Science and psychology cannot themselves save the lost or rescue the abandoned. The Christ of Christianity can. He is the world's one saving, transforming Hope.

Throughout many years I have sought to be His joyful ambassador, a happy announcer of His good news. I have prized the common touch that has enabled me to be the friend of the poor, the confidante of the outcast. I have tried to be gentle with weaklings and generous in judgment with the erring. If a life is to be judged by its fruits in winning many to Christ, in providing homes for the homeless, in placing many on their feet again, finding them work and inducing several of them to enter into the Christian world to live more fully the Christ-indwelling life, and in the strength of His love to go out and labour to repair the old waste places and restore the broken paths for others to walk on, then I have truly and fruitfully lived.

I fervently unite my Christian testimony with myriads of others. Christ is my King. Christ is my Saviour. Christ is sufficient for every need and every problem.

> *Some day the silver cord will break,*
> *And I no more as now shall sing;*
> *But oh, the joy when I shall wake*
> *Within the palace of the King!*
> *And I shall see Him face to face*
> *And tell the story saved by grace.*